TABLE OF CONTENTS

Top 20 Test Taking Tips

1. Carefully follow all the test registration procedures
2. Know the test directions, duration, topics, question types, how many questions
3. Setup a flexible study schedule at least 3-4 weeks before test day
4. Study during the time of day you are most alert, relaxed, and stress free
5. Maximize your learning style; visual learner use visual study aids, auditory learner use auditory study aids
6. Focus on your weakest knowledge base
7. Find a study partner to review with and help clarify questions
8. Practice, practice, practice
9. Get a good night's sleep; don't try to cram the night before the test
10. Eat a well balanced meal
11. Know the exact physical location of the testing site; drive the route to the site prior to test day
12. Bring a set of ear plugs; the testing center could be noisy
13. Wear comfortable, loose fitting, layered clothing to the testing center; prepare for it to be either cold or hot during the test
14. Bring at least 2 current forms of ID to the testing center
15. Arrive to the test early; be prepared to wait and be patient
16. Eliminate the obviously wrong answer choices, then guess the first remaining choice
17. Pace yourself; don't rush, but keep working and move on if you get stuck
18. Maintain a positive attitude even if the test is going poorly
19. Keep your first answer unless you are positive it is wrong
20. Check your work, don't make a careless mistake

Client Interviews and Assessments

Preparation for initial potential client visit

When preparing for an initial client consultation, the personal trainer should have the following items prepared for discussion: necessary documents for the client, expectations for the client, expectations of the personal trainer, accurate pricing for sessions, payment expectations (i.e., when payment is due, and what forms of payment are accepted), and on what terms a client is expected to give notice prior to missing a planned session. For instance, the personal trainer should clearly discuss how soon notice must be given prior to a session being missed before the session fee is forfeited by the client. The trainer must also be prepared to give the client a tour of the fitness facilities and explain whether any equipment is necessary for purchase prior to meeting for the first training session (i.e., proper exercise clothing and footwear, etc.). The client should clearly understand what will happen at the first session and when the paperwork is due, especially if medical clearance is necessary.

Paperwork

The personal trainer must have the client fill out the following paperwork: Health History Questionnaire, Par-Q & You, and a Client Participation Contract. The personal trainer must decide if any other contracts or agreements need to be signed, for instance, a payment agreement form, medical clearance form, etc. All paperwork must be completed prior to exercise testing. If the Par-Q & You and/or the Health History Questionnaire indicate medical clearance is required prior to exercise participation, the trainer must clearly explain this to the client and have the client obtain clearance with a medical clearance form. It is also a professional obligation to let any medical staff intimately involved with a client's ongoing care know about exercise plans.

PAR-Q

PAR-Q stands for Physical Activity Readiness Questionnaire.

The first step in finding out a client's general history, this yes-or-no test is intended to determine whether a person has a cardiorespiratory dysfunction (such as coronary heart disease). It not only alerts the CPT to clients who may need medical attention but it also allows the health and fitness professional to assign clients appropriate activity levels: from low to medium to high.

Questions on the PAR-Q are intended to determine whether a potential client:
- Feels chest pain (at any time);
- Loses balance or consciousness;
- Experiences bone or joint problems;
- Takes medication for high blood pressure or a heart condition;
- Knows of any other reason that he or she should not perform physical activity.

Fitness Assessment

The fitness assessment is simply a tool for gathering information that can be used to gain insight about a client's past, present, and future. After determining a person's health issues and fitness level, the CPT can help a client to shape his or her goals and continually progress through an integrated training program (as well as modify acute variables—important aspects of exercise training that can be changed to fit a particular client's needs).

The fitness assessment is not intended to take the place of a medical exam or to diagnose medical conditions. A health and fitness professional should refer his or her clients to qualified health-care providers whenever necessary. A CPT should not attempt to provide:
Medical rehabilitation;
- Exercises intended to serve as medical treatments;
- Specific diets or nutritional supplements;
- Treatment for chronic diseases or injuries;
- Personal counseling.

Effectively communicating expectations

At the initial client session, the personal trainer must clearly communicate future expectations for the client. Some expectations can include the following: timeliness, dress, and level of exertion/discomfort to be expected. Expectations should be shared in an encouraging way and with positive nonverbal communication, for instance, eye contact, firm but kind tone of voice, smile, etc. The personal trainer should provide an explanation of how goals will be created and assessed in an ongoing fashion. Time should be given for the client to ask questions; the client should always feel free to ask questions at any time and participate in future goal setting.

Proper communication

The personal trainer can communicate through various means with the client. Communication should be maintained on a professional level, yet remain friendly and encouraging towards the client. Communication can take place in the following ways: verbally (verbal instruction), nonverbally (eye contact, tone of voice, gestures), written (newsletters, handouts, articles, brochures), email (updates on progress, session reminders), phone, or text messaging. In communicating with a client, the personal trainer needs to keep in mind principles of confidentiality and share client information only with those for whom written consent has been obtained. Text messaging and phone calls from the trainer's personal phone should be used with care and only when other means of communication are unavailable in order to keep a professional relationship with the client.

Prescreening clients prior to exercise instruction

It is important to prescreen clients in order to assess their medical risk. Once medical risk is assessed, appropriate goals and exercise sessions can be planned. Understanding the client's medical risk factors also helps the personal trainer to know whether medical consent must be given in order to begin training. The most common forms for personal trainer use include the following: health/medical history questionnaire, informed consent, trainer-client contract, and policies/procedures.

- Health/medical history questionnaire: Par-Q & You or general health questionnaire that assesses common risk factors related to exercise and indicates whether medical clearance must be given.
- Informed consent: ensures the client understands the relative risks and discomforts associated with exercise sessions.
- Trainer-client contract: the agreed-upon sessions and pricing, signed by both the trainer and the client.
- Policies/procedures: the agreed-upon procedures and policies necessary to provide a positive experience for clients and ensure their goals are met; can include guidelines for missed sessions, appropriate dress, etc.

Medical clearance

According to the Par-Q & You form, medical clearance is necessary for client participation in an exercise program when one or more questions have been answered with a "yes," the client is over 40, and has been inactive for a substantial period of time. On other health history questionnaires, any condition that is not currently under observation by medical personnel must be noted and recommended to a physician's attention. Depending on the conditions present in the client, written permission from the physician may be all that is necessary; however, certain cardiovascular issues may need to be assessed through a physician-handled stress test. Medical clearance must be obtained prior to the initial exercise testing; however, a client may not have any negative health indicators based on completion of the initial paperwork. A medical issue may arise during the initial exercise testing or in subsequent sessions. If this is the case, medical clearance should be recommended and obtained immediately.

Use of screening information to develop overall goals

Initial screening information includes information gathered from both the paperwork and fitness testing of the client. From the paperwork, the personal trainer understands what are the client's personal goals, level of motivation, and health challenges. From the fitness testing, the personal trainer evaluates physiological deficiencies in the client's training. The client then develops goals with the following criteria in mind: begin with the greatest deficiencies and work down to the lesser ones, connect each specific goal with an area of weakness and clearly show how the goal will strengthen it, make the goal measureable and attainable. Creating a measurable and attainable goal also requires creating a rubric which will assess the client progress at regular intervals.

Subjective assessment

Information and conclusions

Understanding the broad details of a client's personal life can provide details about the way they move throughout their. Subjective information about a person's general history may include his or her occupation, recreational activities, and hobbies.

Knowing a client's daily patterns, the CPT is better able to understand that person's structure and the way their movement functions throughout the day. A determination can then be made about the client's capacity for additional movement. For instance, those who enjoy relatively sedentary activities are not likely to start training at the same level as those who regularly play recreational sports. Likewise, a woman who spends most of her day sitting in front of a computer is likely to have tight hip flexors.

Medical background

The kinetic chain's function is altered by any type of injury or surgery. To determine which activities may be contraindicated for certain dysfunctions, the CPT must ask clients about their medical histories.
Be sure to ask about:
- Injuries and/or pain, including:
  - Sprains of the ankle, groin, or hamstrings;
  - Tendinitis of the shoulders, knee (patellar), shins (posterior tibialis), or arch of the foot (plantar fasciitis);
  - Chronic headaches.
- Surgeries, especially those that:
  - Are performed on the joints (shoulder, back, knee, ankle, or foot);
  - Involve cutting of the abdominal wall (Cesarean section or appendectomy).
- Chronic conditions or diseases, such as:
  - Coronary heart/artery disease or congestive heart failure;
  - Cardiovascular disease or hypertension;
  - High cholesterol;
  - Lung or breathing problems;
  - Diabetes mellitus.
- Any medications.

Medical risk factors

Evidence supports the hypothesis that muscular and skeletal ailments are more prevalent in modern society than they were a generation ago. Many factors contribute to this decline in the health of the average American. An increase in automation and a decrease in physical activity have altered the overall health and physical fitness level of Americans over the last century. A good deal of research has been done on subjects such as:

- Low back pain—This problem is estimated to affect four out of five American adults and is common among those who work in offices and remain seated for long periods of time.
- Knee injuries—There are approximately 100,000 injuries to the anterior cruciate ligament (ACL) each year, with the vast majority resulting from non–sport-related incidents. Most of these injuries occur to young people between the ages of 15 and 25 and may be a result of a less-active population.
- Chronic disease—A decrease in activity can lead to or exacerbate chronic problems such as obesity, diabetes, hypertension, and other heart conditions.
- Kinetic chain injuries—In recent years, these types of injuries ranked near the top reasons for visits to the doctor. These are often caused by poor posture resulting from repetitive sitting and lack of muscle support caused by sedentary lifestyles.

Pharmacological information

While it is never appropriate for a CPT to suggest or administer medications to clients, it is important to know what medications a client is taking and the general effects of those medicines. A summary of common medications and the general physiological effects each might have on the body includes:

- Beta blockers—treat high blood pressure (hypertension) or irregular heart rate (arrhythmia).
- Calcium-channel blockers—treat high blood pressure or angina, which is chest pain caused by inadequate blood flow to the heart.
- Nitrates—treat high blood pressure or congestive heart failure, which results from the heart's inability to adequately pump blood to the body's organs.
- Diuretics—help purge excess water from the body and are often used to treat edema, congestive heart failure, or high blood pressure.
- Bronchodilators—alleviate constriction in the bronchi and bronchioles of the lungs and are often used to treat pulmonary disorders such as asthma.
- Vasodilators—relax blood vessels and are often used to treat high blood pressure.
- Antidepressants—mood elevators and stabilizers often used to help alleviate symptoms of depression and other psychiatric disorders.

Objective Assessment

Five types of objective information

There are five forms of objective information a CPT should gather about a client's general history during the fitness assessment:
1. Heart/lung (cardiorespiratory) efficiency;
2. Dynamic movement (posture);
3. Physiology, including heart rate and blood pressure;
4. Fat and muscle composition, which may include body mass index (BMI) and waist-to-hip ratios;
5. Athletic ability or performance, which may include a bench press assessment and a squat assessment.

Objective information is essential when training a client because it gives a good idea of what a person is presently capable of in terms of beginning a fitness program. Objective information also gives a trainer information from which he or she can compare future results in order to establish progress made by a client and how effective a particular regimen is.

Heart rate

The radial pulse can be felt by placing two fingers on the inside of the wrist in line with (and just above) the thumb. The carotid pulse can be found by placing two fingers along the neck, just to the side of the larynx, right underneath the jawline.

Although resting heart rates vary, men have an average rate of 70 beats per minute, while women have rates of 75 beats per minute on average.

To find an estimated maximum heart rate, subtract the client's age from the number 220.

Blood pressure

Blood pressure is a measurement that reveals how much blood flow force is being placed on the interior walls of a person's arteries. This pressure emanates from the heart, which pumps the blood throughout the body.

Blood pressure is measured by using both a stethoscope (to listen to the pulse at the brachial artery) and a sphygmomanometer (cuffed around the arm, above the elbow).

The cuff should be rapidly inflated to 20–30 mm Hg above the point at which the pulse is no longer felt at the wrist. The pressure should be released at 2 mm Hg per second.

The top number of a blood pressure measurement is called the systolic reading and is measured when the pressure is first released and the sound of the pulse is first heard. It reflects the top level of force produced by the cardiac cycle. The diastolic reading is measured when the sound of the pulse fades away. It appears on the bottom of the reading and reflects the lowest amount of pressure produced during the cardiac cycle.

An average normal reading for an adult is between 120 to 130 mm Hg for the systolic number and from 80 to 85 mm Hg for the diastolic number.

Body fat percentage

<u>Use of skin calipers</u>
The four sites on the body that should be measured with calipers—in millimeters—in order to use the Durnin-Womersly formula. Because it's important to be consistent when measuring skin folds, all measurements should be taken on the right side of the body. The four sites to measure are:
1. A vertical fold of skin on top of the biceps, halfway between the elbow and shoulder;
2. A vertical fold of skin over the triceps, halfway between the elbow and shoulder;
3. An angled fold of skin (of about 45 degrees) at the subscapula, about two centimeters below the inner angle of the scapula;
4. An angled fold of skin (of about 45 degrees) just above the iliac crest and in line with the apex of the armpit.

BMI and waste-to-hip ratio

In order to find a person's waist-to-hip ratio, measure the smallest part of his or her waist and largest part of his or her hips. Divide the waist measurement by the hip measurement. Women whose ratio exceeds 0.80 are at risk of having obesity-related health problems. The same is true for men with ratios greater than 0.95.

To reveal whether a person's weight is appropriate for his/her height, simply divide weight (in kilograms) by height (in meters squared). When a person's BMI exceeds 25, the likelihood of their having obesity-related health problems increases.

BMI is an acronym that stands for body mass index. This measurement is more accurate than weight to determine a person's fitness level and state of overweight or obesity because it takes into account the ratio of height to weight. BMI is also known as the Quetelet index.

BMI does not measure body fat, but it is a useful assessment tool to determine whether a person's weight correlates in a healthy manner to his or her height. To determine BMI, the following formula is used:

Weight (in kilograms) ÷ height (in meters)^2

A person is considered overweight when they have a BMI that exceeds 25. A range of 25 to 30 is considered mildly overweight, while 30 to 35 is moderately overweight. Measurements greater than 35 are considered obese, or severely overweight.

Cardiorespiratory assessments

The three-minute step test and Rockport walk test are both cardiorespiratory assessments that estimate a cardiovascular starting point (which can be modified for a person's ability level).

The three-minute step test is conducted by having a client step up 24 times per minute onto an 12-inch step, for a total of three minutes (72 steps total). After a one-minute rest, the client's recovery pulse should be measured for 30 seconds. By using a mathematical formula, cardiovascular (CV) efficiency level can be rated—poor through very good.

To perform the Rockport walk test, have a client walk on a treadmill for one mile as fast as he or she can remain controlled. At the one-mile mark, quickly record the time and the client's heart rate. Determine the client's VO2 (maximal oxygen uptake) score, and locate it in the Rockport chart.

Movement Assessment

Functional anatomy

Nervous system

<u>Form and function</u>
The nervous system has three main functions:
1. Sensing—perceive alterations to the body, both internal and external.
2. Integrating—compute sensory information in order to communicate to the body the correct action to take.
3. Communicating—transmit information to the muscles of the body when it is time to initiate movement and control this movement.

Because the nervous system controls all human movement, it is important to train it in order to ingrain correct movement and improve reaction time.

<u>Anatomical structure</u>
The nervous system is a complex communication system within the body. It is composed of the central and peripheral nervous systems. The central nervous system includes the main organs of the nervous system: the brain and the spinal column. The peripheral nervous system includes all parts of the nervous system that branch off from the central nervous system, such as cranial and spinal nerves.

The nervous system is made up of billions of neurons—special cells made up of a cell body, axon, and dendrite. The three main types of neurons are separated by the jobs they each perform:
- Afferent neurons—transmit information from muscles and organs to the central nervous system.
- Interneurons—transmit information from neuron to neuron.
- Efferent neurons—transmit information from the central nervous system to muscles or glands.

<u>Mechanoreceptors, muscle spindles, Golgi tendon organs, and joint receptors</u>
Mechanoreceptors can be found in the joints and connective tissues of the body (tendons, ligaments, and muscles). They sense changes in the compression or stretching of the muscles or tissues. Muscle spindles, Golgi tendon organs, and joint receptors are forms of mechanoreceptors.

Muscle spindles are found in the muscles. They sense alteration in the length of the muscle and the rapidity of that alteration. Muscle spindles also have a protective mechanism; when stimulated, they will contract in order to prevent overstretching of the muscle.

Golgi tendon organs can be found at the junction of a muscle and a tendon. They sense alteration in muscle tension and the rapidity of that alteration. Golgi tendon organs also have a protective mechanism; when stimulated, they will relax in order to prevent overstressing the muscle.

Joint receptors are found around the joints. They sense changes in speed in the joint. Joint receptors also have a protective mechanism; they help sense when a joint is in an overextended position and reflexively respond to protect that joint.

Skeletal system

The skeletal system, which consists of approximately 206 bones, gives the body its architecture. The skeletal system is the foundation for human movement, the form upon which our muscles rest, and a protective system for our organs.

The skeletal system is divided into two major sections: the axial skeletal system and the appendicular skeletal system. The axial skeletal system is composed of the head, spine, and rib cage and has nearly 80 bones. The appendicular system comprises the appendages along with the shoulders and hip complex. It has more than 120 bones.

The skeletal system has two main functions when it comes to motion. The first is to provide support. The second is to act as levers propelled by muscle force.

<u>Bone markings</u>
Every bone has certain markings on its exterior that serve various functions. One major function is to act as a place where muscles or other connective tissue can attach. There are two major categories of bone markings: processes and depressions.

Processes are bulges that come out from the bone. Some examples include the rounded ends of the femur or humerus. Listed here are examples of bone processes:
- Trochanters—the rounded end of the femur; the hip bone is also known as the greater trochanter.
- Tubercles—the top of the humerus; there are tubercles in the shoulder complex also.
- Condyles—the bottom of the femur, where condyles help form the knee joint.
- Epicondyles—the bottom of the humerus, where epicondyles help form the elbow joint.

Depressions are parts of the bone that are smooth or flat. Common depressions are fossa or sulcus. These are locations where muscle or body tissues can attach or pass between.

<u>Joints</u>
A joint is a juncture where bones meet that can bend or move. Joints can be categorized by how they move or by their physiology.
The motion of a joint is called arthrokinematics. Joints can move in three ways:
1. Spin—the joints rotate on top on one another. This happens at the elbow.
2. Roll—one joint rolls across the other. This happens at the knee when it bends, with the femur rolling across the tibia.
3. Slide—one joint skids across the other. This happens at the knee when it bends, with the tibia sliding along the femur.

There are two major types of joints, designated by physiology: synovial and nonsynovial:
- Synovial joints are those pulled together by a system of ligaments, which give these types of joints greater range of motion. Some specific types of synovial joints include ball-and-socket joints (such as the hip joints), hinge joints, and pivot joints.
- Nonsynovial joints have no system of ligaments and can have very little range of motion. Examples include some of the flat joints of the skull and some of the nonmoving joints in the ankle.
- Ligaments are the main connective tissue between a joint and a bone.

Muscular system

The muscular system is the part of the body that connects the nervous system and the skeletal system to produce actual motion and movement. The nervous system generates communication that tells the body's muscles to perform a certain action, and the muscles generate the necessary force to move the skeletal system to accomplish that action.

Skeletal muscles comprise a network of muscle fibers that are bundled together like thick wires wrapped in a casing. The outer casing is known as the fascia.

The connective tissue that anchors the muscles to the bones is called a tendon. Tendons are similar to ligaments in that they have a low supply of blood and are vulnerable to longer recovery time when injured.

<u>Muscle fibers</u>
Muscle fibers are very complex cells that are unique in the body. Each cell is encompassed by plasma called the sarcolemma and has all of the typical elements of a cell. However, muscle fibers have an additional feature: myofibrils, which contain thick and thin filaments (actin and myosin) that give the muscle fiber cell its ability to contract.

These two types of filaments create a grid known as a sarcomere. A sarcomere is basically analogous to a neuron, acting as the basic building block of the muscular system.

Two vital protein structures that affect muscle contraction are troponin and tropomyosin, both located in the actin filament. Troponin provides a place for tropomyosin and calcium, both essential to muscle contraction, to bind. Tropomyosin blocks myosin from binding in order to keep the muscle relaxed.

There are different types of muscle fibers that can accomplish different tasks. They fall into two primary groups:
1. Type I muscle fibers—also known as slow-twitch muscle fibers, or red fibers, due to their high hemoglobin capacity. These muscle fibers have a higher blood-flow capacity and thus higher oxygen delivery and can handle longer-term strain. They are smaller in size than fast-twitch muscle fibers.
2. Type II muscle fibers—also known as fast-twitch muscle fibers, or white fibers, due to their low hemoglobin capacity. These muscles have a lower blood-flow capacity and can move quickly and with more force, but tire faster. They are larger than slow-twitch muscle fibers.

All muscles contain both slow- and fast-twitch muscle fibers, but the ratios of each of the different fibers vary according to the overall function of that particular muscle.

Muscle groups
There are four major categories of muscles, differentiated by the primary function of that type of muscle:
1. Agonists—create a primary movement. They are therefore also known as prime movers. The gluteus maximus is an agonist muscle when performing a squatting movement.
2. Antagonists—counteract the actions of agonist muscles. The psoas muscle performs the opposite action as the gluteus maximus when performing a squatting movement.
3. Synergists—act at the same time as an agonist muscle to assist in the primary movement. The hamstrings are the synergist muscles when performing a squatting movement.
4. Stabilizers—stabilize and support agonist muscles while they perform a primary movement. The transversus abdominis stabilize the body during a squatting movement.

Lower leg complex
Anterior tibialis—runs along the outside of the tibia from under the knee to the ankle. It helps stabilize the foot.
Posterior tibialis—runs along the back of the tibia, under the fibula. It helps control the foot.

Soleus—the fleshy part of the back of the lower leg. It also runs down the sides of the Achilles tendon. It controls walking motion in the leg and ankle and supports the foot.

Gastrocnemius—on the back of the leg below the knee. It works with the soleus to control walking and stabilize the foot.

Peroneus longus—runs along the tibia on the outer part of the leg. It flexes and everts the foot.

Hamstring complex

Biceps femoris (long head)—emanates from the pelvis and inserts at the top of the fibula. It is essential in knee and hip movement.

Biceps femoris (short head)—runs along the lower part of the back of the femur. It is essential to knee and tibia movement.

Semimembranosus—runs along the back femur, through the center of the leg. It is essential to hip, knee, and tibia movement.

Semitendinosus—runs along the back of the femur toward the inner thigh. It is essential to hip, knee, and tibia movement.

Quadriceps complex

Vastus lateralis—runs along the outside of the front thigh. It stabilizes the knee and controls all movement for that joint.

Vastus medialis—runs along the inner thigh close to the knee. It is essential to all movement for the knee joint.

Vastus intermedius—runs along the vastus lateralis, the length of the front thigh. It is also essential to all movement for the knee joint.

Rectus femoris—runs down the center of the front thigh. It is also essential to knee motion and stability.

Hip musculature complex

Adductor longus, adductor magnus (anterior fibers), adductor magnus (posterior fibers), and adductor brevis—fall under the pelvis, interwoven at the top of the femur. Together, they control hip adduction, abduction, flexion, and rotation.

Gracilis—runs along the interior of the top of the femur. It is also essential to all elements of hip movement.

Pectineus—runs along the back edge of the upper part of the femur. It is also essential to all elements of hip movement.

Gluteus medius (anterior fibers), gluteus medius (posterior fibers), gluteus minimus—run along the outer edge of back of the pelvis. Together, they control hip adduction, abduction, flexion, and rotation.

Tensor fascia lata (TFL)—runs along the top of the outer part of the hip. It is essential to hip flexion, abduction, adduction, and rotation.

Gluteus maximus—the fleshy part of the buttocks. It affects hip rotation and extension as well as stabilizing the lumbo-pelvic-hip (LPH) complex.

Psoas—run along the top of the hips to the base of the lowest vertebrae. These muscles are essential to hip movement and the rotation of the lumbar spine.

Sartorius—runs across the top of the thigh from the outer hip to the inner thigh. This muscle affects both hip and knee function.

Piriformis—rests along the front of the sacrum. It affects hip movement and also helps to stabilize hip joints.

Abdominal musculature

Rectus abdominis—run along the midline of the abdomen. They affect and control all core motion.

External oblique—run down the sides of the torso. They affect and control all core motion.

Internal oblique—run under the external obliques along the sides of the torso. They affect and control all core motion as well as stabilize the lumbo-pelvic-hip (LPH) complex.

Transversus abdominis—run along the side of the torso up and across under the ribs. They help stabilize the internal organs and the LPH complex.

Diaphragm—runs underneath the rib cage. It pulls open the thoracic cavity to accommodate oxygen intake.

Muscles of the back

Superficial erector spinae—the following muscles run down the length of the spine. Together they control spinal movement and stabilize the spine during activity:
- Iliocostalis;
- Longissimus;
- Spinalis.

Quadratus lumborum—runs along the lower back and connects to the top of the pelvis. It affects spinal flexion and also stabilizes the lumbo-pelvic-hip (LPH) complex.

Transversospinalis complex

Semispinalis—the following muscles run from the bottom of the back of the skull to the top of the shoulders and spine. Together they control the movement of the upper spine as well as the head:
- Thoracis;
- Cervicis;
- Capitis.

Multifidus—run along the spine down into the sacrum. They control spinal flexion and lower-hip rotation.

Muscles in the shoulder

Latissimus dorsi—runs across the back under the scapula. It is critical to shoulder movement.

Serratus anterior—run around the rib cage underneath the armpit. They affect the movement of the scapula.

Rhomboids—run across the top middle of the back, just under the neck. They also affect the movement of the scapula.

Lower trapezius, middle trapezius, and upper trapezius—run along both sides of the spine from the base of the neck down. They are also essential to all aspects of movement of the scapula.

Levator scapulae—runs along the side of the neck down to the top of the shoulder. It affects the up/down motion of the scapula.

Pectoralis major—runs along the front of the chest. It is essential to all movement of the shoulder complex.

Pectoralis minor—connects the front of the shoulder to the top ribs. It pulls the scapula forward.

Deltoid—the fleshy muscle that runs along the top of the arm. It is essential to all shoulder movement.

Biceps brachii—runs along the top length of the humerus. It is essential to shoulder and elbow movement.

Triceps—runs along the bottom of the humerus, or the back of the upper arm. It is essential to shoulder and elbow movement.

Muscles in the rotator cuff

Teres minor—runs along the lateral edge of the scapula. It accelerates and decelerates shoulder rotation.

Infraspinatus—sits under and along the scapula. It accelerates and decelerates shoulder rotation.

Subscapularis—covers the back along the scapula. It accelerates and decelerates shoulder rotation.

Supraspinatus—runs along the interior of the top of the shoulder. It helps accelerate abduction and decelerate adduction of the arm.

Teres major—runs along the chest to under the armpit. It is essential to shoulder rotation and movement.

Muscles in the neck

Sternocleidomastoid—run from the side of the back of the head down to the cervical collar. They help control movement of the head and cervical spine.

Scalenes—run down the sides of the neck at the shoulders. They help stabilize and control the movement of the cervical spine.

Longus coli—run along the sides of the cervical vertebrae. They help control the movement of the cervical spine.

Longus capitis—runs along the side of the neck. It helps stabilize and move the cervical spine.

Cardiovascular system

The cardiovascular system comprises the elements in the body that create and circulate blood including the heart, the blood, the veins, and the capillaries.

The heart muscle is the primary organ of the cardiovascular system. It pumps oxygenated blood to the body. It has four distinct chambers (two atria and two ventricles) and two pumps. The atria collect the blood as it returns to the heart, with the right atrium collecting deoxygenated blood coming in from the body and the left atrium collecting oxygenated blood coming in from the lungs. The ventricles pump the blood to the body.

Heart rate is how fast the heart pumps, usually measured at rest. The average adult has a resting heart rate of between 70 and 80 beats every minute.

Stroke volume is how much blood the heart pumps out in each beat. The average adult has a stroke volume of between 75 and 80 milliliters per beat. This is a more complex measurement to make than heart rate.

These two measurements combine to reflect the performance capability of the heart. This is referred to as cardiac output.

Blood and channels of blood distribution
Blood is the liquid that flows throughout the body, carrying oxygen and nutrients to all body systems. It also acts as a conduit to rid the body of waste products. The average person has about 1.5 gallons of blood circulating at one time, and blood makes up just less than 10 percent of a person's overall weight.

Blood has various functions in the body. First and foremost, it acts as a transportation conduit, taking oxygen and essential nutrients to all areas of the body. Second, it regulates the body, helping keep temperature constant and maintaining acid balance. Third, it is a defensive mechanism, clotting when necessary to prevent bleeding and creating and circulating defensive cells to help fight infection.

Blood flows away from the heart in arteries, which branch into arterioles and then into even-smaller capillaries. It returns to the heart via the veins.

Respiratory system

The respiratory system encompasses all of the organs and systems that provide for breathing; it is also called the pulmonary system. The primary purpose of the respiratory system is to support cell function by bringing oxygen into the body and ridding the body of waste products such as carbon dioxide. The respiratory system includes the lungs and the cardiovascular system, which moves the oxygen through the body via the blood.

Breathing is the process of inhaling oxygen (inspiration) and exhaling its waste product, carbon dioxide (exhalation). Inspiration requires the muscles to work while exhalation is an involuntary, reflexive action.

The respiratory pump is the entire respiratory physiology, located in the chest and body. It includes both hard and soft tissues (bones such as the sternum and ribs) and muscles such as the diaphragm and the sternocleidomastoid.

Respiratory process
The respiratory process operates in the following order:
1. Oxygen is inhaled through the nose and/or mouth and down the trachea;
2. The oxygen passes into the bronchi;
3. The oxygen fills the lungs and alveoli;
4. The blood is pumped into the heart;
5. The blood is pumped into the lungs;
6. The blood is infused with oxygen;
7. The oxygenated blood is pumped back into the heart;
8. The oxygenated blood is pumped throughout the body.

The efficient delivery of oxygen depends on both the respiratory system and the cardiovascular system working in synergy. This process is called oxygen consumption, denoted using VO2. The formula for determining oxygen consumption is:

VO2 = cardiac output (which is heart rate × stroke volume) × a – v O2 (which is the difference between the oxygen content of arterial blood versus venous blood)

Oxygen and energy
Oxygen is necessary when any activity will last longer than 30 seconds. These types of activities are termed aerobic activities, meaning they require oxygen. Activities of shorter duration that do not need an influx of oxygen to be sustained are called anaerobic activities. Both types of activities still require adequate energy, whether using oxygen or not.

Energy is the fuel needed for the body to run. The study of how this fuel is converted from food and nutrients into mechanical energy is called bioenergetics. The conversion is only the beginning, however. Once the energy has been converted, it must be sent through a conductor mechanism to a place where muscles can use it. The most common conductor mechanism is adenosine triphosphate (ATP).

ATP is composed of adenine, ribose, and a series of phosphates. The body can make ATP in three ways, which are together referred to as the bioenergetic continuum: without the use of oxygen (anaerobic), with the use of oxygen (aerobic), or through the oxidative pathway.

Dysfunctional respiration
Breathing is the foundation for all movement and cardiovascular efficiency. Disruption in proper breathing or glitches in the physiology of breathing can affect

overall health and act as an impediment to proper training. It can also herald a more-widespread problem with the movement continuum.

Stress and anxiety can affect proper breathing. Altered breathing can result in:
- The wrong muscles being used to breathe;
- Muscles needed to support the spine and skull can be overused, resulting in tension and headaches;
- Breathing too much can lead to an improper oxygen ratio (hyperventilation).

These problems can be precursors to sleep disorders, psychiatric problems such as heightened anxiety, and headaches.

Anatomical terms

Superior—above a given point.
Inferior—below a given point.
Anterior (ventral)—of or pertaining to the front part of the body.
Posterior (dorsal)—of or pertaining to the back part of the body.
Proximal—more closely related to the center of the body.
Distal—the farthest point away from the center of the body.
Lateral—the farthest point away from the midline (line bisecting the body from head to toes).
Contralateral—on the opposite side of the body.
Ipsilateral—on the same side of the body.
Medial—closest point to the midline of the body.

Functional Biomechanics

Biomechanics is the field of study that contemplates the workings of the kinetic chain, from the movements it makes to the forces that act internally and externally upon it. Important elements of biomechanics include joint motion, the movement of muscles, force, and leverage, among other concepts.

Human movement can be looked at as an interrelated cycle that encompasses the nervous system, the skeletal system, and the muscular system:
- The central nervous system (CNS) collects information from the internal environment;
- The CNS collects information from the external environment;
- The CNS processes this information;
- The information passes through to the muscles;
- The muscles move the skeletal system.

Kinetic chain

The kinetic chain refers to the system of bones, joints, and muscles connected through the nervous system that allows the human body to move. The health and stability of the kinetic chain directly correlate to how well a person can move and the level of ease or discomfort this may cause.

Because the kinetic chain is made up of several different body systems, each must be fully functional for optimal movement. Imbalance or impairment to any system or element of a system can have a significant effect on movement. This makes it very important for a CPT to understand each aspect of the kinetic chain and address each particular client's needs in his or her training.

Planes of motion

Optimal training techniques use exercises that span all three planes of motion. While many movements use mainly one plane of motion, no movement occurs solely in one plane. The best way to visualize these planes is by picturing a pane of clear glass passing through the body:
- Frontal plane—The pane of glass passes through the body from the head to the toes, bisecting the body into front and back halves.
- Transverse plane—The pane of glass passes through the center of the body at the abdomen, bisecting the body into top and bottom halves.
- Sagittal plane—The pane of glass passes through the body from the head to the toes, bisecting the body into right and left halves.

Types of motion

There are many different types of motions the body can make. Knowing the terminology can help to quickly and efficiently define these movements.
- Adduction—movement in toward the center of the body.
- Abduction—movement away from the center of the body.
- External rotation—movement of a joint away from the center of the body.
- Internal rotation—movement of a joint in toward the center of the body.
- Pronation—rotation out of either the radioulnar joint or subtalar joint.
- Supination—rotation in of either the radioulnar joint or subtalar joint.
- Extension—the straightening out of a joint to increase its angle.
- Flexion—the bending of a joint to decrease its angle.

Muscle actions

There are three main muscle actions that can be produced:
1. Concentric muscle action—A concentric contraction results in a muscle being shortened—when the muscle is exerting more force than what is presently being placed on it.
2. Eccentric muscle action—An eccentric contraction results in a muscle being lengthened—when the muscle is exerting less force than what is presently being placed upon it. Eccentric contractions are also called negative, meaning force is being put on the muscle. This is often seen when a muscle is returning to its original position or decelerating.
3. Isometric muscle action—The muscle is exerting the same amount of force that is being placed upon it—when the muscle is stabilizing and balancing.

Muscular force

These terms help define the interrelation of the kinetic chain and musculoskeletal system and how force and energy come into play in terms of human movement. Understanding these terms increases a health and fitness professional's ability to recognize and describe movement and impairments and improve a client's training regimen.
- Muscular force—describes the interplay between two objects that creates a speeding up or slowing down of one or both objects. Force can be categorized in terms of the level of force, or how much force there is, and which direction it emanates from or continues in.
- Length-tension relationships—the optimum length for a muscle at which it can achieve its top force. Hyperextension and underextension do not allow the muscle fibers to work at their peak capacity.
- Force-velocity curve—the ability of muscles to produce more force at a higher rate of speed.
- Force-couple relationships—the synergistic relationship between certain muscles and muscle groups that result in the movement of an entire joint. This often includes a pushing and pulling action on the joint.

Motor control

Motor control is the body's ability to control the elements of the kinetic chain based on the information it collects from internal and external sources. In order to increase motor control, it is important to train each element individually and also in an integrated manner to manipulate motor behavior, or the body's response to internal and external stimuli.

Muscle synergies (the way muscles interact and work together), proprioception (how the body interprets incoming sense information), and sensorimotor integration (the process of the nervous system in processing sense information and translating it into motion) all come into play in affecting motor control. Each of these components features the interaction of more than one body system. Increased efficiency of each will positively affect overall motor control.

Integrating motor behavior and control

Motor learning is the method by which motor behavior and motor control are honed. Motor learning refers to the way repetition and practice can essentially hardwire movement into the body's neuromuscular pathways.

There are two main forms of sensory feedback: Internal feedback is information that comes from the body via posture, force-couple relationships, and so on and is integrated into the body's own motor learning; external feedback is information that comes from an exterior source, such as watching oneself in the mirror or working with a trainer, that a person can incorporate into adjusting motor learning.

There are two main forms of external feedback: Knowledge of results comes after a movement is completed and gives insight as to the end result of the motion; knowledge of performance also comes after a movement, but gives insight as to tweaks that could be made to the execution of the motion.

Flexibility concerns

Postural distortions come from muscle imbalances that lead to improper posture, which in turn results in poor movement coordination and ultimately results in injury. Poor flexibility can result in relative flexibility, a state in which the kinetic chain adapts to improper posture or other body distortions in an effort to move in the easiest way possible. This results in a hardwiring of sorts, in which the body learns to move improperly along the wrong lines, manifesting in many different movements that are actually compensations for the proper use and movement of a muscle or joint.

One example is when a person rotates his or her feet outward while performing squats. If there was actual flexibility instead of relative flexibility, the person would have enough extensibility in the ankles to allow for a clean squat. However, since it is likely that this person has overactive calf muscles, he or she must compensate for the lack of flexion in the ankles by putting the feet further apart and rotating them out.

Biomechanical assessments

Movement assessments can provide information on postural distortions. These can be caused by overactive or underactive muscles. These are descriptions of assessments, and which muscles are causing the problems:

Overhead squat assessment

Knees that buckle inward are evidence of
Overactive muscles:
- Adductor complex;
- Biceps femoris;
- Tensor fascia lata (TFL);
- Vastus lateralis;

Underactive muscles:
- Gluteus medius;
- Gluteus maximus;
- Vastus medialis oblique.

An arch in the lower back at the lumbo-pelvic hip (LPH) complex is evidence of
Overactive muscles include:
- Hip flexor complex;
- Erector spinae;

Underactive muscles:
- Gluteus maximus;
- Hamstrings;
- All intrinsic core stabilizers (such as the transverse abdominus, multifidus, transversospinalis, internal obliques, and pelvic-floor muscles).

The overhead squat assessment is used by CPTs to determine a client's total body strength and dynamic flexibility.

Single-let squat assessment

Knee moving inward is evidence of
Overactive muscles:
- Adductor complex;
- Biceps femoris;
- Tensor fascia lata (TFL);
- Vastus lateralis;

Underactive muscles:
- Gluteus medius;
- Gluteus maximus;
- Vastus medialis oblique.

The single-leg squat assessment is used by CPTs to determine the stability of a person's hip joint, ankle flexibility, and center strength. It may not be appropriate for elderly or obese individuals, who may find it too difficult to perform.

Pulling assessment

An arch in the lower back at the lumbo-pelvic-hip (LPH) complex is evidence of
Overactive muscles:
- Hip flexor complex;
- Erector spinae;

Underactive muscles:
- All intrinsic core stabilizers (such as the transverse abdominus, multifidus, transversospinalis, internal obliques, and pelvic-floor muscles).

Pulling up of the shoulders is evidence of
Overactive muscles:
- Levator scapulae;
- Sternocleidomastoid;
- Upper trapezius;

Underactive muscles:
- Mid trapezius;
- Lower trapezius.

A head that juts forward is evidence of
Overactive muscles:
- Levator scapulae;
- Sternocleidomastoid;
- Upper trapezius;

Underactive muscles:
- Deep cervical flexors.

Strength assessments

Davies and shark skill tests

In order to give a Davies test, the client should begin in a push-up position with the hands positioned one yard (3 feet) apart. The client rapidly moves one hand to touch the other and returns to the push-up position. Have the client alternate sides. See how many touches can be done in a 15-second time period. Repeat three times.

The Davies test is designed to evaluate upper-body strength, agility, and stability; it may not be appropriate for people with shoulder problems or injuries.

In order to give a shark skill test, create a square grid on the floor with nine boxes, perhaps with masking tape. Start the client in the center box. Have the client stand on one leg with her hands on her hips. Have the client hop from the center box to square one, then to the center, then to square two, then to the center, and so on, until she has hopped into each square. Switch legs and repeat the exercise. Do this four times, twice for each leg, recording the time for performance. Add one-tenth of a second for mistakes, such as the raised foot falling to the ground, stepping into an incorrect square, or the hands dropping.

The shark skill test is designed to evaluate lower-body strength and agility as well as a person's muscle coordination; it may not be appropriate for people with lower-extremity problems or injuries.

Postural and movement dysfunctions

Deconditioned states

Deconditioned states refer to the decline or lack of physical fitness characterized by low stamina, decreased strength, muscle distortions, lack of flexibility, and lack of overall muscle stability and agility. A deconditioned state is not merely being overweight; rather, it describes an overall decline in physical ability, from musculoskeletal strength and capability to cardiorespiratory capacity and beyond.

In order to increase fitness, it is important to go beyond typical training programs in a safe and steady manner. Often, typical training programs initiated for sedentary individuals substantially increase their risk for injury and muscle overwork.

Proprioception is the information transmitted through the body via the senses. A training program that incorporates movements throughout the different planes of motion and through all muscle actions and contractions increases the level of neuromuscular communication throughout the body. This results in a proprioceptively enriched environment that forces the body to increase its ability to stabilize and balance. This can be accomplished by using a stability ball when doing any number of training exercises.

Postural distortion

A postural distortion is a muscle imbalance that results in the improper use of muscle groups. This can manifest in many ways, including various body parts being misaligned or improperly supported.

A common postural distortion for the upper extremities is when a person's arms slant forward. This indicates the pectoralis major muscle is tight or overactive. The rhomboids are likely weak or underactive along with the mid- and lower trapezius and the rotator cuff.

A common postural distortion for the LPH complex is an anterior pelvic tilt. This indicates the psoas muscle is tight or overactive. The gluteus maximus and hamstrings are likely weak or underactive.

Cumulative injury cycle

Postural distortions coupled with repetitive motions, even just those of daily living, result in the kinetic chain not working properly. This affects muscles and connective tissue and confuses the body, which reacts as though these distortions are injuries that need to be repaired. It will therefore try to fix the problem, resulting in the cumulative injury cycle.

This cycle includes the following:
- Muscle imbalance;
- Injury to connective tissue;
- Inflammation of the injured tissues;
- Increased muscle tension and spasms;
- Knots in the soft tissue (also called adhesions);
- Altered reciprocal inhibition;
- Increased synergistic dominance (when synergist muscles overcompensate for a weak prime mover muscle);
- Altered joint motion.

If not caught and repaired, this cycle can lead to permanent changes in the body. Davis's law states that soft tissue will form or rebuild itself along the lines of any stress, which may run contrary to the natural lines of a muscle. This will inhibit optimal muscle function.

General adaptation syndrome

Hans Selye identified general adaptation syndrome, which states that the body, specifically the kinetic chain, attempts to stay in equilibrium at all times by counteracting any stresses placed on it. There are three types of responses to various stresses:

1. Alarm reaction—This reaction to a stress mechanism results in the protective system of the body being set into motion.
2. Resistance development—The body has become familiar with the stress mechanism and has begun to develop specific responses to handle and adapt to the stress.
3. Exhaustion—This occurs when the body has been overwhelmed by a stress mechanism and can no longer cope. This can result in damage to the body ranging from emotional wear to physical damage such as stress fractures or muscle tears.

Muscle imbalance

Muscle imbalance is nonoptimum lengthening or shortening of a muscle around a joint, which causes improper movement. This can be the result of any distortion of the kinetic chain, such as an improper length-tension relationship or force-couple relationship. When there is a muscle imbalance, instead of muscles working together synergistically as they are designed to, one muscle or muscle group works harder than it should, resulting in overactivity or tightness, while another muscle or muscle group works less than it should, resulting in it being underactive or weak. This can lead to postural distortion and injury.

Muscle distortions can be caused by:
- Repetitive motions;
- Emotional stress/heightened emotional states;
- Stress on the body that affects the kinetic chain;
- Cumulative trauma;
- Poor nervous system and muscle communication/coordination;
- Lack of strength;
- Improper physical training.

Altered reciprocal inhibition

Altered reciprocal inhibition refers to an overactive or tight agonist muscle that stifles the proper function of its partner antagonist muscle—as with a tight hip flexor reciprocally inhibiting its antagonist muscle, the hip extensor.

Synergistic dominance occurs when synergist muscles overcompensate for a weak prime mover muscle. This is the body's backup system, allowing the muscles adjacent to a main muscle to take up the slack when it is not functioning optimally.

Both synergistic dominance and altered reciprocal inhibition result in muscle imbalances that affect the kinetic chain.

Arthrokinetic dysfunction refers to alterations to the kinetic chain that change the way joints work. It can also lead to muscle imbalances and other postural distortions.

Neuromuscular efficiency

Neuromuscular efficiency refers to the body's ability to properly communicate correct movements in response to various stimuli to the nervous system and the muscular system.

Muscle spindles and Golgi tendon organs, key sensory organs that affect neuromuscular control and efficiency, react to changes in the muscles and have protective mechanisms that react to extreme movement. Muscle spindles can detect changes in the length of a muscle and also how quickly the muscle changes. Golgi tendon organs can sense tension alterations in a muscle and how quickly this tension changes.

Flexibility training can help challenge these organs in a positive way, increasing neuromuscular efficiency. When these body parts are stimulated for a set amount of time (say with a 30-second stretch), the result is autogenic inhibition, an automatic response from the receptors that tells the body to relax the muscle and allow for more stretch.

Program Design and Implementation

Exercise risks and benefits

Exercise guidelines for otherwise healthy adults include the following: in general, adults should do fitness-related physical activity 3–5 days per week, do leisure-related physical activity 2–3 days per week, and sit sparingly. The following exercise guidelines refer to seniors: in general, they should acquire 30 minutes of moderate physical activity on most if not all days of the week and should consult a physician before moving to a more vigorous program. Flexibility and resistance training should be included on several days each week. For children, the following guidelines are applicable: have at least 60 minutes and up to several hours of physical activity that is age appropriate on most to all days of the week. Activity should be moderate to vigorous and should take place in 15-minute increments. Activities lasting longer than 2 hours should be discouraged. For women who are pregnant, the following guidelines apply: moderate physical activity should be accumulated on most to all days of the week if there are no contraindications to exercise present. In addition, regular exercise is encouraged; if a woman was previously sedentary, light intensity exercise is encouraged. Exercise in the supine position is discouraged after the first trimester.

It is important to understand the risks and benefits of exercise for adults, seniors, children/adolescents, and pregnant women because it allows the personal trainer to know what she can incorporate for exercise testing and prescription purposes. These guidelines serve as a road map for the trainer and client to see what the acceptable norms are for exercise. Knowledge of the risks and benefits helps the trainer know what will be most appropriate for the client for each session.

Clients medically cleared to exercise with chronic disease

Many patients have a chronic disease but have been advised by their doctor to exercise. In such cases, specific guidelines apply to their exercise prescription. Patients who have arthritis are encouraged to perform cardiorespiratory training 3–5 days/week (20–60 min, large muscle groups), resistance 2–3 days/week (1 set of 3–20 repetitions, 8–10 exercises), and flexibility 5–7 days/week ideally (15–30 sec per stretch, all the major muscle groups, 2–4x each). Patients with diabetes mellitus are encouraged to perform cardiorespiratory training 3–4 days/week (20–60 min), resistance (2 days per week minimum with 48 hours of rest in between, 1 set of 15–20 repetitions for each major muscle group), and flexibility (every day ideally). Patients with dyslipidemia are encouraged to perform cardiorespiratory training 5 or more days/week (40–60 min, primarily large muscle group aerobic activities), resistance 2–3 days/week (1 set of 3–20 repetitions, 8–10 exercises), and flexibility 5–7 days/week ideally (15–30 sec per stretch, all the major muscle groups, 2–4x each). Hypertensive patients follow a similar protocol as those with dyslipidemia with the following alterations: cardiorespiratory activity on 3–7 days/week (30–60 min), and resistance training should be in combination with aerobic activity using lower resistance and higher repetitions. For obese patients, cardiorespiratory training should begin initially with a moderate intensity, 45–60 min/session on 5–7 days/week. Obese patients may use resistance guidelines that apply to otherwise healthy adults.

Individuals with metabolic syndrome may use the same guidelines as otherwise healthy adults unless there is a negative immune response to exercise; otherwise adequate rest may be needed prior to continuing. Individuals with osteoporosis should incorporate the following: resistance activities 2 days/week with the load directed over the long axis of the bone (1–2 sets of 8–10 repetitions), flexibility training on most to all days of the week, and cardiorespiratory activity that is not high impact. Individuals with peripheral artery disease should have an extended warm-up (5–10 min) and walking should be the main form of cardiorespiratory activity (3–5 days/week). Resistance training should be complementary to other activity, not instead of the activity. Patients with pulmonary disease should have a minimum of 3–5 days/week of cardiorespiratory activity, and resistance guidelines are the same as otherwise healthy adults.

Physiological responses during exercise that may require a physician

If a client experiences any of the following responses during exercise, the personal trainer may want to refer her to a physician: angina or angina-like symptoms, excessive drop in systolic blood pressure when workload remains constant, shortness of breath and/or excessive cramping in the legs, lightheadedness, confusion, nausea, cyanosis, heart rate does not increase even though exercise intensity increases, an obvious change in heart rhythm. Any of these symptoms could indicate something more serious, and should be referred to a physician for follow-up.

Modifications during initial fitness assessment

Certain clients may require modifications in order to complete the initial fitness assessment. If a client has a disease that affects his range of motion or ease of movement, it may be more beneficial to modify assessments or skip some assessments because the risk of injury outweighs the benefit to the client. In addition, clients who are obese may not be able to complete assessments for muscular endurance and strength or flexibility due to their weight. In such cases, it is acceptable to begin with the recommendations allowed for their population group.

Functional fitness and sports-specific training

Functional fitness refers to fitness exercises that easily translate to real life experiences and help avoid injury in those situations. For instance, for a client who experiences low back pain whenever she does things during the day that require twisting of the spine, it is helpful for the personal trainer to incorporate movements that require twisting of the spine through different planes of movement and with varying resistance modalities to strengthen that area and train it in a new movement pattern. Sports-specific training emphasizes speed, strength, power, and endurance in athletic situations and also includes training specific to the sport in which the client participates. The average client does not necessarily need to engage in sports-specific training.

Balance training

Balance training becomes more important as clients age, and is especially important if clients have diseases such as arthritis. Balance can be included as a separate section of the workout, or if the client is more advanced, it can be combined with other exercises. An example of balance training can be to simply balance on one leg for a certain amount of time. An example of a combined balance and resistance move could be to do a one-legged bicep curl. In addition, balance can be included in cardiovascular training by having clients walk up and down stairs without the use of the railing or walking backwards on an indoor track. Modifications for balance exercises can include providing support for the client by allowing him to hold on to the personal trainer's arm, wall, or railing.

Sports-specific training in power and strength

Sport-specific training for power tends to emphasize explosive movements. This can be achieved through jump training (plyometrics) and through resistance training. Such examples would include jumping hurdles or doing jump squats, and using lighter weights but lifting as quickly or "explosively" as possible. Understanding the anaerobic system allows the personal trainer to work for the goal of power more effectively by utilizing rest periods to full capacity. Strength training involves methodically increasing weight while doing fewer repetitions in order to gain strength. For sports-specific strength the entire body is worked, but the muscles needing to be strengthened for sports performance are given special attention.

Anaerobic vs. aerobic training

Aerobic training uses oxygen to convert food nutrients (primarily carbohydrates) into usable energy. Any time exercise continues after 2 minutes, the aerobic system kicks in. The anaerobic system is the first responder to exercise, and it also converts food nutrients (primarily carbohydrates) into a fuel source, but it does not use oxygen to do so. Anaerobic exercise can refer to short bouts of activity and includes resistance and plyometric training. Aerobic exercise tends to refer to endurance activities such as running or bicycling.

Precautions to take during extreme weather conditions

When extreme weather conditions are present, special care should be taken if exercise testing or training must take place outside. If conditions are hot and humid, it is important that the clients are well-hydrated prior to beginning exercise and are given plenty of opportunities to re-hydrate during exercise. They should be wearing clothing that is moisture-wicking and avoid wearing cotton if at all possible. Clients should be given adequate rest periods. Clients should be observed for signs of heat stroke or heat exhaustion. When conditions are cold and humid, the same instructions apply but with a few modifications. Clients should layer clothing that is moisture-wicking so they can remove it as their body warms up. Additionally, the warm-up should be lengthened to warm up the muscles adequately. In either situation, personal trainers should monitor the clients closely, as they will not always be assertive when they need hydration or if they feel light-headed or dizzy.

Training at moderate and high altitudes

At higher altitudes, it is important to ensure that clients remain hydrated. When a client feels cold, she may not necessarily feel thirsty. Higher altitudes can quickly cause dehydration if the client is waiting until she feels she needs a drink. Feelings of fatigue can also be increased as less oxygen is binding to the hemoglobin molecules in the client's blood. Frequent breaks may be in order, and if the client is traveling to moderate or high altitude and intends to exercise, she must be aware that she may not be able to exercise at the same capacity. She also needs to schedule water breaks even when she is not thirsty. It is important to drink water throughout the day so she is adequately hydrated for her exercise session.

Recording client progress

Recording client progress at the end of each exercise session gives the personal trainer a small picture of how the client is doing from session to session. At the time of reassessment and re-testing, the trainer can then compare results with session notes. This gives both the trainer and the client a full picture of progress. In addition, if keeping in contact with a cooperating physician, it is necessary for the personal trainer to provide ample documentation for liability reasons and so the physician stays as informed as possible.

Choosing appropiate exercises for specific goals

The personal trainer bases each exercise session around one or more of the client goals. With primary goals, it may be necessary to center the entire session around that one goal. With secondary goals, it may be effective to group them together for a session. The client will be more invested in each workout if he knows what goals are being worked on and why. If he can see how the exercises he is doing will help him reach his goals, he will also have increased motivation to continue faithfulness to the exercise routine.

Program design and session and long-term goals

Program design must be specific to where the client's current level of fitness lies. It will not be a beneficial experience for either the client or the trainer if session goals and long-term goals do not match. Session goals should be building blocks that help the client reach the overall goals and thus must be closely related to the overall goals. The program design must properly reflect both the session and overall goals. It is beneficial for the trainer to recognize in both written and verbal form the specific goals for each session.

Interval, continuous, and circuit training programs

Interval training for cardiovascular fitness involves changing speed or grade at various time intervals at which the activity is performed. Continuous training involves staying at a similar speed or grade throughout the entire activity, and circuit training combines cardiovascular and resistance training. Each of these three types of training can be advantageous for cardiovascular fitness. For individuals who were previously sedentary, continuous training is helpful when it is maintained at low to moderate intensities because it will build their endurance, encourage weight loss, and condition their heart rate. Interval training can provide challenges and increase caloric expenditure while still training the client's cardiovascular system. Circuit training combines resistance activities with cardiovascular activities and helps build strength as well as endurance. The drawbacks to these types of training are similar to anything else; if continued for too long, clients will reach a plateau in their performance. Additionally, if one is emphasized over the others, cardiorespiratory fitness or muscular fitness may suffer.

Interval and circuit training could be disadvantageous for a client if the primary goal is to increase her endurance. When doing these types of activities, the client may have to stop the exercise sooner than if a continuous mode of activity was used because the intensity is more difficult. If endurance is the primary goal, it should be attended to first. As endurance increases, interval or circuit training may become more appropriate to include in the training regimen.

<u>Energy systems used</u>
In continuous training, the aerobic system is the primary responder. It is also the primary energy system used in interval training, provided there is no break taken between intervals. With circuit training, either the anaerobic or aerobic system can provide the primary source of energy. When circuit stations are done for less than 2 minutes with at least 30 seconds to 1 minute of rest between stations, anaerobic

pathways supply the energy through the ATP-PC and glycolytic pathways. If stations are rotated with less rest, or clients stay at the station for more than 2 minutes, the aerobic system becomes the primary energy pathway.

Rest within circuit training

In circuit training, rest performs a very important function if the goal is to tax the anaerobic system and cause it to be the primary function. The rest periods between stations cause the anaerobic system to "reload" and be ready to function in the next set of exercises. It is important for the personal trainer to understand that rest plays a large part in the training of the anaerobic system.

Relation of ADLs to long-term fitness goals

When the personal trainer is assessing and creating long-term client goals, it is important to assess how the client feels about his normal life activities. The personal trainer can question him about his leisure time, whether he feels he is physically able to do what he enjoys, or whether any common activities (i.e., sitting or standing for long periods of time) cause unnecessary discomfort. The personal trainer must incorporate exercises that address these issues as they directly correlate to the client's quality of life. Increasing his quality of life allows the client to see that exercise can enable him to do what he enjoys, and it helps him desire to continue seeing those benefits. Activities of daily living can have both short- and long-term goals that relate to them.

Activity and training recommendations for different goals

For general cardiovascular and strength benefits, clients can use the following general guidelines for cardiovascular and muscular fitness and flexibility. For losing weight, it is recommended that clients expend at least 2000 kcal per week in physical activity. For gaining weight, clients need to focus on resistance training for hypertrophy. In addition, for both clients who wish to lose weight and who wish to gain weight, diet plays an important role. In losing weight, caloric ingestion must be regulated and decreased from when they were sedentary. In gaining weight, caloric ingestion must be increased, but it must come from nutritious foods. To improve fitness level and increase athletic performance, clients can focus on specific variables, such as hypertrophy, power, endurance, and speed training as best fits their personal goals. The key with this type of clients is to make sure each workout is challenging and not too comfortable for them.

Advanced methods of resistance training

When a client has given evidence that she is ready for advanced forms of resistance training, the personal trainer can introduce methods such as super sets, Olympic-style lifts, plyometrics, pyramid training, drop set training, contrast training, complex system, lactate tolerance system, or negative set system. Only when the client has moved easily from easy to complex movements in traditional resistance training models should she move on to more difficult resistance training. Olympic-style movements train clients for quick, explosive movements that lift heavier weights. Plyometrics, also known as "jump training," trains for speed and power through different styles of explosive jumps. Pyramid sets begin with high volume and low weight, then increase to low volume with high weight through each subsequent set. Drop set training is a system that uses the same exercise performed to volitional failure in one set, then the weight is lowered and the exercise is repeated. Contrast training combines strength and power training by completing one exercise until volitional failure; a similar movement is then per-formed with a lighter weight but faster pace. Complex training com-bines agonist/antagonist exercises to fatigue a certain muscle in or-der to encourage hypertrophy. The lactate tolerance system has the goal of finishing a predetermined workout in the shortest amount of time possible. The negative set system encourages the exerciser to lift a heavier weight than normal, control the eccentric contraction, and have a spotter assist her with the concentric contraction.

Fitness components related to motor skill

Agility refers to a client's ability to explosively perform several different power movements one after another and in opposing directions; for example, zigzagging. Balance refers to a client's ability to control his body position while either standing still or moving. Reaction time means the client is able to react quickly to exercise stimulus or verbal instruction and change his movement pattern accordingly. Speed is quickness of movement, and power refers to explosive contractions of the muscles. Coordination is the client's ability to do all the aforementioned components so that effective movement occurs.

Contraindications for squats, planks, reverse crunches, and plyometrics

If a client has bad knees or shoulders or back, is morbidly obese, and is unfamiliar with exercise in general, the following types of exercises should be avoided: squats, planks, reverse crunches, plyometrics. Clients need to be started with exercises that are simple before moving on to exercises that are more complex. In addition, clients may need the extra core support that standard resistance machines give before moving on to body-weight exercises that are unsupported. Beginning with these sorts of exercises increases the risk for unnecessary injury.

Contraindications for yoga, PNF, static stretching

Yoga might be contraindicated if the client has greatly reduced flexibility, has an injury, or has had joint or back surgery. In these instances, it is wise to consult the client and assess whether the potential benefit would outweigh the risk. PNF or static stretching might be contraindicated for the client if joints are inflamed; if stretching causes excessive pain; or if she currently has an infection, a vascular or acute injury, joint instability, or a disease that affects the tissue being stretched. If in doubt, consult medical personnel before beginning a stretching regimen.

Contraindications for high-intensity, high-impact cardiovascular exercises

High-intensity, high-impact cardiovascular exercises should be avoided in clients if they have a chronic disease that compromises their joints, an acute injury, acute infection or sickness, or if in general the client has any physical issues that may be exacerbated by beginning a high-intensity regimen. For most clients, moderate physical activity is sufficient for health benefits and disease reduction. The personal trainer must assess the benefits/risk ratio for his client.

Recommendations for overall fitness

Healthy adults and seniors
In general, the client should engage in cardiorespiratory activity 3–5 days/week, resistance training 2–3 days/week, and flexibility (ideally) 5–7days/week. Each activity should emphasize the major muscle groups. Cardiorespiratory training should occur ideally at a range of 12–16 on the RPE scale, and resistance exercise should occur at a range of 19–20 RPE with the intent to reach volitional failure. Stretches should be held for 15–30 seconds each, with each muscle group being stretched 2–4 times at each session.

Healthy children and adolescents
Children should accumulate 60 minutes to several hours of moderate and vigorous physical activity on most days of the week. There should be several periods of activity during the day that last 15 minutes or more, and all activities should be age appropriate. Extended periods of activity that last longer than 2 hours are not encouraged during the day due to heat considerations.

Healthy pregnant women
In pregnant women who are healthy, 30–40 minutes of physical activity on most to all days of the week are encouraged. Women who were sedentary prior to becoming pregnant can begin an exercise regimen that is light. Exercise in the supine position after the first trimester should be avoided due to slightly obstructed venous return that lowers cardiac output and could cause orthostatic hypotension.

Adults with cardiovascular disease but medically cleared to exercise
If clients have a chronic heart disease that is stable, they generally need an extended warm-up (5–10 minutes), resistance exercises 2 days/week that include all the major muscle groups (clients should perform 1 set of 10–15 repetitions to moderate fatigue and use 8–10 different exercises; weight should be increased at a rate of 2–5 lbs per week for arms and 5–10 lbs per week for legs), and cardiovascular activity 3–4 times weekly (in addition to an increase in daily total energy expenditure) that is moderate intensity. For the greatest benefits, 5–6 hours of cardiovascular activity

per week is recommended. Stretching all the major muscle groups (15–30 sec each, 2–4 stretches per muscle group) daily is encouraged.

Adults with metabolic syndrome but medically cleared for exercise
For clients who have a metabolic syndrome but are medically cleared for exercise, their goals should include the following: cardiorespiratory activity 3–4 days/week, lasting 20–60 minutes, at an intensity of 50–80% of their HRR. Resistance training should emphasize lower resistance and lower intensity: 1 set of 10–15 repetitions for each of the major muscle groups, increasing to 15–20 repetitions. Stretching of all the major muscle groups (15–30 sec each, 2–4 stretches per muscle group) should be emphasized on a daily basis.

Adults with chronic pain and arthritis but medically cleared to exercise
For adults who suffer from arthritis or other joint pain, their exercise prescription is as follows: cardiorespiratory (3–5 days/week, 20–60 min duration, large muscle groups emphasized), resistance (2–3 days/week, 1 set of 3–20 repetitions, 8–10 total exercises that cover all the major muscle groups), flexibility (preferred: 5–7 days/week, 15–30 sec each, 2–4 stretches for each major muscle group). Overstretching should be discouraged; morning exercise depends on a client-by-client basis, based on whether they find it helpful or not.

Importance of accurate medical history

For clients who are pregnant, children and adolescents, and the generally healthy population, it is always necessary to have an accurate medical history. This decreases the personal trainer's liability by allowing her to prescribe exercise that will avoid exacerbating medical issues. The trainer will also understand what medications the client is on and how they may impact exercise. Additionally, the personal trainer will be aware of potential triggers for worsening any existing medical conditions.

Exercise modifications

When an exercise is too challenging or not challenging enough, the personal trainer should give a modification that will make it more appropriate for the client. It is the personal trainer's responsibility to observe the client and ask questions to make sure the intensity or the type of exercise is appropriate for the client; some clients have a "pain is gain" mentality and may not volunteer that the exercise is too difficult for them. Likewise, clients new to exercise may not realize if an exercise is too easy for them; they may simply appreciate that they don't feel horrible as they exercise. The personal trainer must educate her clients on the benefits of an appropriately challenging workout.

Components and appropriate flow of an exercise program

An exercise session should start up with an adequate warm-up of the large muscle groups that will also increase the heart rate and prepare the body for what is to come. Depending upon the client, static stretches may be appropriate after the warm-up. Resistance activity should come next, so the client is not too fatigued to be paying attention to proper technique, appropriate weight choice, and personal trainer cues. Next should come cardiovascular activity, followed by a cool-down, and static stretches.

Exercises for major muscle groups

The following exercises would be appropriate for the major muscle groups: chest (push-ups), upper back (double arm row), abdominal muscles (abdominal curl-ups), lower back (good morning), quadriceps group and hamstring group (weighted squats), calves (calf raises), shoulders (shoulder raises), biceps (biceps curls), and triceps (triceps dips).

Monitoring response to exercise

During exercise, there are various ways that a personal trainer can monitor a client's response to exercise. The RPE scale is an efficient way of assessing whether the workload is too challenging or not challenging enough for the client. Paying attention to physical signs of distress, such as labored breathing, pallor, dizziness, or sharp pain, can also be indicators that something more serious may be occurring.

Maximum heart rate and heart rate reserve

In order to find the maximum heart rate, simply take the client's age and subtract it from the number 220. The resulting number is the age-adjusted maximum heart rate. To find the heart rate reserve (HRR), take the client's age and subtract it from 220. Take the resulting number, and subtract the resting pulse from it. This is the heart rate reserve. If training according to a percentage of the client's heart rate reserve, multiply the HRR by the percentage desired for training, then add the resting pulse to it. **Example:** A 60-year-old client needs to be trained at 70% of his HRR, his resting pulse is 65: 220 – 60 (age) = 160 (age-adjusted maximum heart rate); 160 – 65 (resting pulse) = 95; 95 x .70 = 66.5 + 65 (resting pulse) = 131.5 bpm. This client should have the goal of 131 bpm for training at 70% of his HRR.

Target heart rates for different medical considerations

Depending on the chronic condition that the client has, a specific training zone will be based on her HRR. Cardiac patients should have a goal of training up to 85% of HRR. For managing hypertension, training from 40% to 70% of HRR is recommended. For clients with arthritis, it is recommended to train within 50% to

85% of HRR. Diabetic clients should train within 50% to 80% of HRR. For clients with dyslipidemia, it is recommended to train within 40% to 70% of their HRR. For obese clients, initial exercise should have the goal of being within range of 40% to 60% of HRR; progression to higher intensities (50% to 75% of HRR) is recommended. For clients with osteoporosis, it is recommended to pursue non-impact activities at 40% to 70% of HRR.

Periodized training

Periodized training allows the personal trainer to focus on goals such as endurance and hypertrophy with a client while avoiding overtraining. For example, a period of 12 weeks can be broken down into 3 periods of 4 weeks in each period. Through these different periods, the trainer varies the client's intensity, frequency, and duration of exercise so that a plateau is not reached, but maximal hypertrophy and endurance is attained. Chance of injury is reduced because the client is rotating training styles and also which muscles are receiving the most training. Periodized training also helps those clients concerned with increasing different exercise variables such as speed, strength, and power.

In a periodized training schedule, the personal trainer can vary the goal within each period so that muscular power, hypertrophy, endurance, and strength can be achieved without reaching a plateau. For the goal of power, high-intensity, short-interval exercises should be included with the goal of most movements being explosive rather than static. Moderate-intensity sessions should be in between the power sessions to promote recovery. For hypertrophy, resistance training should be with a moderate-intensity weight, 10–15 repetitions, with rest of 30–60 seconds between sets. Endurance activities can be coupled with hypertrophy training and should be between 30–60 minutes for 4–6 days per week at moderate intensity, or 30–60 minutes 2–3 days per week for higher training intensities. Strength training should be done with higher resistance than hypertrophy training. The goal should be 2–3 sets of 6–8 repetitions, where the client feels tired with the last 2 repetitions. Additionally, exercises should be specific to the client's sport goals if they have any.

Repetition maximum test

The 1 RM test measures the greatest amount of resistance that the client can move through a full range of motion while still in control of the weight. This can provide a measure of either upper body or lower body strength. The benefit of knowing the client's 1 RM allows the personal trainer to more accurately estimate submaximal resistance loads with which to begin training. An example of the 1 RM test for the upper body is a bench press; an example of the 1 RM test for the lower body is the leg press.

Resistance exercises to build strength

Resistance exercises can help build muscular strength and endurance. When using the proper types of exercises, a client is able to more easily complete activities of daily living, deter rapid bone loss, and reduce the risk for joint disease. Resistance training works along with cardiovascular training to decrease fat mass and increase lean mass. Resistance exercises break down the muscles by creating micro-tears in the tissue; the proper recovery period helps to rebuild those tissues and increase strength and hypertrophy.

Effects of cardiovascular training on activities of daily living and endurance activities

Cardiovascular training helps the heart to pump blood more effectively. As such, resting heart rate begins to lower and resting blood pressure begins to lower. During exercise, heart rate and blood pressure take longer to increase as the body becomes more efficient with the workload. Clients will notice the longer they are committed to an exercise routine, the more daily activities they will be able to complete with less pain or fatigue involved. Clients will also notice better quality of sleep and feel more energetic. For endurance activities, clients will notice that they can exercise for longer periods of time, increase their speed, and overall adapt to training stimulus more quickly.

Effects of exercise on motor skills and coordination

As clients exercise, they will notice a positive effect on motor skills and coordination. With specific training in each of the following areas: resistance, flexibility, cardiovascular, and balance, clients will have increased quality of life. Coordination and motor skills are improved when speed and balance activities are included in the training regimen. Balance training can be incorporated in resistance training (e.g., completing a bicep curl while standing on one leg) or in cardiovascular activities (e.g., power skips or bicycling) and trains clients to use their fine and gross motor skills to complete the movement. The more movements are practiced in an exercise session, the more efficient clients will become in performing them, and their motor skills and coordination will continue to improve.

Demonstration of expected movement patterns

To ensure the client understands exactly what to do for an exercise, the personal trainer needs to physically demonstrate the movement pattern as well as provide verbal and nonverbal cues. It is never appropriate for the trainer to assume the client understands based on verbal instruction alone. An example of a verbal cue is to give instructions for how to complete an exercise. An example of a nonverbal cue would be personally demonstrating the exercise or helping the client complete the movement.

Demonstration of proper range of motion

Demonstrating proper range of motion helps the client to remain free from injury. One resistance exercise that is often done incorrectly is the lat pull. People will typically pull the bar down behind their neck and head. Although the glenohumeral joint can rotate 360 degrees, it is not advisable to train by bringing the arms behind the head in this manner. Proper form requires lowering the bar in front of the face and neck but not leaning back away from the bar. Performing this exercise improperly often leads to overuse injuries in the shoulder joint that could become serious enough for medical attention.

Benefits of using several different resistance modalities

Using several different resistance training modalities allows the trainer to see what the client enjoys the most. This also gives the client a taste of the variety resistance training can offer. Additionally, muscles can be trained in different ways depending on the goal of strength, hypertrophy, endurance, or power, and it becomes less likely that a plateau will occur for the client. Examples of different resistance modalities include the following: variable resistance devices, static resistance devices, kettle bells, dynamic constant external resistance devices, etc. It is necessary for the personal trainer to always keep her eyes on the client during the performance of each movement. Spotting is appropriate and requires verbal and nonverbal cues to ensure the client is performing each movement as safely as possible.

Nontraditional resistance training activity

For some clients, nontraditional resistance training may be in order; this can include stability balls, balance boards, resistance bands, medicine balls, and foam rollers. These pieces of equipment are useful for clients who are rehabilitating from injury, are elderly, are incapacitated in any way, or need to work on their balance. Additionally, it provides a way to change a movement and make it more complex so as to increase the intensity of the workout for clients. Using this type of equipment is also considered functional training and helps clients achieve ease of movement and greater strength in activities of daily living.

Dangers of the Valsalva maneuver

The Valsalva maneuver occurs when a client holds his breath during a resistance or cardiovascular exercise. This is dangerous because it causes a sharp increase in blood pressure and heart rate which can lead to the client becoming light-headed or dizzy and passing out. Clients need to learn to breathe appropriately during cardiovascular exercises and during the eccentric and concentric phases of resistance training in order to avoid the Valsalva maneuver.

Biomechanics of resistance training, yoga, and running

In resistance training and yoga the spine will move through all planes of movement in a variety of ways including bending, twisting, and stretching and will also move through the frontal, sagittal, and transverse planes. Yoga uses almost exclusively isometric training, while resistance training may utilize isometric or isokinetic training. Both resistance training and yoga can exert compressive forces on the spine, and care must be taken to protect vulnerable areas. During running, the spine should stay relatively stable with little to no twisting and no bending or stretching, and should only move through the frontal plane. Compressive forces will also be present for the spine during running activities. Joints may go through flexion, extension, circumduction, abduction, adduction, or hyperextension for running, yoga, and resistance training.

Negative effects when training is ceased

If a client stops training for an extended period of time, her muscles begin to atrophy, and gains that are made in both the cardiovascular and muscular systems are lost. Clients may begin to notice that they have aches and pains returning and that range of motion becomes more limited. They will lose the ability to complete with the least amount of effort tasks that require increased levels of coordination and may become short of breath with a lower amount of exertion. When they begin training again, clients can increase their abilities and functional performance within the cardiovascular and muscular systems. The rule of thumb is "if you don't use it, you lose it."

Overtraining

The following are signs that the client may be overtraining: fatigue, moodiness, unenthusiastic about workouts, difficulty sleeping at night, and irritation. If these signs are obvious in the client to a great extent, it may be necessary to refer the client to a physician. Overtraining can result from a desire to get in shape faster by exercising longer and harder than is necessary and not utilizing rest periods. It can also be the result of poor self-image or an eating disorder. It is necessary for the personal trainer to educate the client on the dangers of overtraining and how it can be avoided.

Improper form and technique

Using improper technique and form, whether performing cardiovascular or resistance-type activities, can be detrimental to a client's health. It can cause overuse or acute injuries, both of which impede a client's progress in reaching his health goals. Injury may give a client misgivings about continuing an exercise routine and lower his motivation to become healthy if he feels he is just going to be injured. Additionally, improper technique lessens the benefit of the activity being done because the muscles are not being trained in an appropriate fashion. Also, inappropriate motor patterns for the movement are recorded in the client's mind, and he will have to "unlearn" the wrong technique in order to learn the right technique. It is always more beneficial to learn the correct technique the first time.

Appropriate exercise clothing

When exercising in outdoor conditions, the client must pay attention to the appropriate clothing for outside temperatures. If it is hot and humid outside, cotton is not an appropriate clothing choice because it will not wick away excess moisture from the skin. It is best to avoid wearing a hat, as that will also hold in heat. When exercising in a cold environment, the client must layer her clothing and have a moisture-wicking layer closest to the skin. As she gets hot, she can remove clothing accordingly. The appropriate tennis shoe must also be chosen for whether cardiovascular exercise is prescribed or whether speed or resistance training is prescribed. A thinner-soled shoe is required for plyometric or resistance training, and is also more helpful for training in balance issues.

Learning styles

It is important for the personal trainer to remember that the client may not have a learning style that corresponds with his own. In such circumstances, the trainer needs to be informed on how best to train that client in a way that will make sense with her learning style. For instance, a kinesthetic learner may need to not only have verbal instructions, she may need to do a practice try of the movement before actually beginning a set. Additionally, a visual learner will learn best by watching the trainer go through a complete range of motion with the movement, and an auditory learner will rely heavily on verbal cues.

Properly spotting a client

When spotting a client, the personal trainer must stand either behind, beside, or in front of the client. The appropriate position is dependent on the movement being completed. The trainer should ask permission prior to touching the client; all touch should be professional and with the intention of providing assistance for the movement if necessary.

Determining whether an exercise session should end or continue

If a client is working at an intensity higher than is beneficial for him, it can be evidenced by labored breathing, inability to talk, flushed face, or complaint of sharp pain. If an exercise is stopped, the personal trainer needs to assess whether the client can continue working out after a short break. If client heart rate lowers significantly and client feels able to continue, exercise can continue. If the client still feels faint or exasperated following the break, the session may need to be terminated.

Normal and abnormal response to exercise

In a healthy adult, the normal response to exercise is increased heart rate and blood pressure as blood is shuttled to the working muscles. In an adult with chronic health issues, heart rate and/or blood pressure may rise too quickly and cause negative symptoms that may cause the exercise session to be terminated. The personal trainer must make sure adults with chronic conditions begin exercising according to their appropriate protocols.

Improper use of cardiovascular equipment

One example of improper technique when using cardiovascular equipment would be hunching over from the waist or gripping the bar on the treadmill. Both of these issues can cause poor posture and reduce the number of calories being used. Additionally, the client may become light-headed or dizzy because she is compressing her diaphragm by leaning over, which leads to insufficient breath intake and thus hyperventilation to get more air and oxygen to working muscles.

Improper technique for resistance machines, free weights, and stability equipment

When doing any type of resistance activity, form must be prioritized in order to avoid injury. With a resistance machine, any movement that causes the client to arch his back would be an example of improper technique and may indicate that he is using too much weight. For free weight exercises, if the client struggles to complete the move in general, or begins to lean backward in order to complete the movement, this is also improper technique. With stability equipment, any time it is used for something other than its intended purpose to promote balance, it is being used improperly.

Improper stretching techniques

An example of improper technique for partner stretching would be for the partner to force a muscle to stretch farther than it is capable of stretching due to muscle tightness or impaired range of motion. With static stretching, the client must be sure to hold the stretch rather than bouncing in the stretch, as this would promote muscle injury. With dynamic stretching, it would be improper for the client to move a joint outside of its normal range of motion in order to heighten the stretch.

Assessment of client understanding

There are various ways that a personal trainer can assess the client's understanding of the movement patterns. Once the trainer has finished demonstrating and instructing the client on how to do a specific exercise, she can ask if what she has said makes sense. Additionally, she can ask if the client has any questions prior to beginning the exercise. Finally, it will become clear during the course of the movement whether the client has understood the instructions and demonstration. If he performs the movement improperly, he lacks clear understanding of what was asked of him.

Effective communication of proper technique and feedback

When giving feedback to a client regarding proper technique for exercise, the personal trainer should utilize as many avenues as possible to communicate. The trainer can verbally explain the proper technique needed. He should follow this with a demonstration of the movement pattern. The client should then attempt the movement pattern one time without any additional weight or resistance of any kind. As the client is performing the movement, the personal trainer should be spotting her and providing verbal cues the entire time. Throughout the process, the client should be allowed to ask questions and encouraged to do so. When giving feedback regarding client performance, the trainer should begin with what the client has been doing correctly so far and any ways she has improved since the initial exercise testing. Additionally, once the trainer has given feedback to the client, the client should be allowed to ask questions. In areas where the client is still deficient in performance, the trainer should share with her a plan for improvement.

Modification of exercise programs for healthy individuals

For pregnant women, if any absolute contraindications are present, exercises may not be an option for them. If any of the relative contraindications are present for a pregnant woman, modifications will be necessary to her typical routine. Additionally, as she progresses further into her pregnancy, her center of gravity shifts forward, requiring exercise to be modified for comfort. For adults, seniors, children, adolescents, and pregnant women, exercise may be modified for an acute injury or sickness, extreme discomfort associated with an exercise, or extreme temperatures. If a client is dehydrated, exercise should be stopped altogether.

Benefits of modifications for clients with chronic disease

When clients with chronic disease are cleared to exercise, modifications may be necessary for a variety of reasons. When first beginning an exercise routine, clients may need extra modifications in order to feel successful with what they are doing. As they progress through their workout plan and begin to meet their goals, exercises may have to be modified to become more challenging to reach future goals. Modifications also provide a range of choices for clients so they can have some autonomy in choosing parts of their workout routines. Additionally, clients who are exercising under doctor's orders must be given a progression of exercise that takes their recent medical history into account. Heart rate should be regularly monitored, and their level of exertion (using the Borg RPE scale) should be closely followed also.

Avoiding training plateaus

Specificity
Specificity of exercise refers to training that upholds a specific goal; for instance, strength training requires different protocol than speed training. When training for strength, an example of specificity would be to create a particular goal for each session that focuses on strength for a certain area. One session might focus on core strength, while the next focuses on lower body strength. Specificity helps to avoid a training plateau because the personal trainer is keeping track of when the client reaches the training goals for strength in a particular area. Once this goal is reached, a new goal can be made, with the training sessions specifically corresponding to it.

Progressive overload
The term progressive overload refers to progressively overloading a bodily system for the purpose of exercise training. For instance, one way of achieving progressive overload for endurance cardiovascular training would be to increase distance run by a half-mile per week. This helps the client to achieve the overall goal of a specific distance while also training the cardiovascular system to function more efficiently. However, since the distance is being increased, it keeps the body from becoming overly efficient and expending fewer calories at a distance that becomes too comfortable for training purposes.

Proper progression of exercise sessions
In order to reach the client goals at all, the personal trainer must continue to pay attention to proper progression of exercise from simple to complex. If training remains simple for the client, major cardiovascular and muscular gains will not be made. Additionally, a training plateau will occur once the body becomes overly efficient with an exercise routine. Changing one or more exercise variables (overload, specificity, duration, frequency) will allow the training plateau to be overcome.

Proper progression for developing strength in chest and legs

A proper exercise progression goes from simple to complex, single-joint to multi-joint exercises. As an example, proper progression for strength development in the chest might be as follows: assisted bench press on a resistance machine, bench press with free weights and an exercise ball, push-ups, burpees. For strength progression in the legs, an example of a proper progression would be seated leg extension, seated leg press, squat, side shuffle to a squat. The personal trainer should spot the client at each point of the progression.

Periodized training program to increase or maintain athletic performance variables

Periodized training programs are valuable because they allow training plateaus to be overcome, and they can be used to train an athlete for various parts of athletic performance. For example, the first period of training might be for strength and general cardiovascular fitness. The second period of training could be for speed and sport-specific skills with maintenance strength training. The third period of training could include the sports season, with maintenance for speed, strength, and sport-specific skills. The fourth period could include recovery, with limited endurance and strength training, while increasing exercise load towards the end of the period to prepare for the first period again.

Feedback regarding client's experience and assessment of progress

The personal trainer can gain an idea of the client's perspective of his training success through a variety of different ways. The trainer can verbally address the client and ask whether he sees he is meeting goals or not. The trainer can also create a checklist or survey for the client to fill out when goals are reassessed. At the end of the training, the personal trainer can ask the client to fill out a satisfaction survey to indicate the overall success of the program in his perspective.

Reviewing current goals and creating new goals

The personal trainer should assess the client goals at frequent intervals throughout the exercise program. For instance, if the client has contracted to work with the personal trainer for 40 sessions, it might be good to assess some of the minor goals every 5 sessions, while assessing the main goal(s) every 10 sessions. This gives enough time for change to take place, but the assessments are close enough together for the client to have the goals in mind during each workout. Once a goal is met, a new goal should take its place. The personal trainer and the client should both keep a log of when the goals are met and when new goals are created.

Progression and Modifications

Extrinsic and intrinsic reinforcement strategies

An extrinsic reinforcement strategy is an external way of rewarding or reinforcing positive client behavior. For example, if a client has recently reached a goal of losing 5 lbs, the trainer can positively reinforce and reward the client reaching the goal by giving her the opportunity to engage in only her favorite fitness activities for one session. An intrinsic reward or reinforcement would increase self-esteem; using the same example, if a client lost 5 lbs, her intrinsic reinforcement would be the increase in self-esteem.

Increasing client motivation to achieve fitness goals

Personal trainers can help clients reach fitness goals by working patiently with them, reminding them of their progress, and showing them objectively how they are reaching their goals. Trainers can also motivate clients by giving them rewards or awards for reaching their goals. Trainers can encourage clients to identify who can be a part of their social support network. Understanding how to motivate clients will enable the clients to be more faithful in reaching their goals.

Helping clients increase physical activity outside of exercise sessions

The client often understands the need to increase energy expenditure throughout the day in addition to the structured exercise sessions but may need help in understanding how to do this. The personal trainer can help by having the client describe a typical daily routine and then make suggestions on how to increase levels of activity. For example, the personal trainer might suggest the client take the stairs to the office instead of the elevator, park a little farther from the office entrance than normal, or take 5 minutes every hour of work to walk around the office a few times.

Healthy lifestyle

The personal trainer is very instrumental in helping the client understand what options are available for a healthy lifestyle. The personal trainer can take time at each session to discuss with the client the choices he has made throughout the week and how he can be more effective by choosing healthier options. The personal trainer becomes a mentor, source of accountability, cheerleader, and coach for the client and must encourage honest communication so the client can receive the best results of his programming.

Lifestyle management techniques and health coaching principles

One example of a lifestyle management technique is to have the client keep a food log and an activity log each week. The trainer can take the logs, make suggestions, and return the logs to the client to help promote change. Another example is to help the client identify sources of stress in her life and help create alternatives for managing it. Anytime the client can help in creating solutions to issues that stand in the way of well-being and health, the more likely she will be to follow through on the course of action.

Persistence

Long-term success requires persistence, or the ability to continue on a path even in the face of problems or challenges. This holds true for fitness goals as well—not only accomplishing the goals in the first place but also maintaining the results over time. By addressing this reality with clients, it is more likely that they will be able to take some setbacks as just part of a realistic journey toward the goal, and not allow these challenges to completely derail the ultimate goals.

Research has shown that even among people who can keep their annual resolutions for two years, they admit to more than a dozen cheats in that period of time. However, instead of becoming completely demoralized, they viewed this as a realistic part of life and resumed their drive to maintain the goal.

Learning

Learning deals with how a client can gain knowledge from the positives and negatives he or she has experienced on the road to meeting goals. ACE advocates self-monitoring, which simply means that the client monitors his or her own progress, honestly viewing and recording both the good and the bad. Studies have shown that people who engage in self-monitoring are better able to meet their goals.

Recording helps the client see progress or slipups more clearly. Once the client can see his or her progress as objectively as possible, he or she can enter into course correction, which means the client makes adjustments to both strategy and execution, tweaking the overall routine to incorporate more of what works and to avoid things that are not working or are having little benefit in terms of achieving the overarching goals.

Methods of learning

It is vitally important that a client be aware of actions or activities that do not help accomplish a goal and learn to change in order to correct them. If a client continues with activities that are contrary to accomplishing a goal, progress may be slow or nonexistent and the client may become discouraged or feel like they are failing: two eventualities a trainer definitely wants to avoid. ACE recommends the following:

- Change what you can—It is important to work on things that can be changed and let go of what cannot. Look at actions, not measurements, when beginning a fitness regimen.
- Look at the record—When a client examines his or her personal record of activities and habits, eating and health patterns (both positive and negative) emerge. Use this information as a tool to restrategize.
- Rate it—Have clients rate their daily progress on a 0–10 scale.
- Look at progress—Review clients' training records with them to monitor progress toward fitness goals.

Belief

Belief is an essential element in working toward goals. No matter how specific a person's vision is and what strategy is undertaken to accomplish it, it will never come to fruition if the client does not actually believe that it is possible to accomplish the goals. Sometimes, a person may say they want something, but he or she will have an underlying fear of achieving it. These conflicting attitudes can lead to apathy or self-sabotage.

As a health and fitness professional, it is important to work toward minimizing a client's fear, uncertainty, and doubt. Identifying these elements with the client is the first step. In order to build the client's confidence, small, achievable goals should be used. Any negative feelings can also be indulged in a controlled manner; for example, the client may be allowed one minute in the locker room to verbalize his or her fears or impediments and then leave these feelings at the door for the duration of the workout.

Research

There is a great deal of scientific information available relating to how a sense of believing in oneself can actually have a great positive impact on a person's life. These impacts include:

- Having a better work ethic.
- Being more content.
- Tackling problems in a positive manner.
- Recovering from setbacks more easily.
- Coping better and learn from mistakes.
- Having better goal-setting skills.

Effective communication of proper technique and feedback

When giving feedback to a client regarding proper technique for exercise, the personal trainer should utilize as many avenues as possible to communicate. The trainer can verbally explain the proper technique needed. He should follow this with a demonstration of the movement pattern. The client should then attempt the movement pattern one time without any additional weight or resistance of any kind. As the client is performing the movement, the personal trainer should be spotting her and providing verbal cues the entire time. Throughout the process, the client should be allowed to ask questions and encouraged to do so. When giving feedback regarding client performance, the trainer should begin with what the client has been doing correctly so far and any ways she has improved since the initial exercise testing. Additionally, once the trainer has given feedback to the client, the client should be allowed to ask questions. In areas where the client is still deficient in performance, the trainer should share with her a plan for improvement.

Feedback can be given to a client in a variety of ways. Evaluative feedback helps the client know what she is doing correctly and incorrectly in the movement pattern ("You are doing a great job of not allowing your knees to go past your toes, but make sure your toes are pointed forward."). Supportive feedback is a means of encouraging the client, perhaps through a difficult part of the workout ("I know it's tough, but we're almost through. Do you think you can finish 2 more laps?"). Descriptive feedback is clear and concise feedback that provides correction at the end of a movement pattern or session ("In future squat-type exercises, I want you to focus on squeezing the muscles of your gluteus to decrease pressure on your knees."). Feedback should be given to the client verbally at regular intervals, but also in written form when she is regularly evaluated for goal assessment.

Communication with clients

There are various ways of communicating information with a client, and the personal trainer must find out which types of communication will be most beneficial for the client. Talking with the client over the phone is most beneficial if the client can be reached easily via telephone, although the personal trainer needs to understand the protocol of the fitness center for making such calls from her personal number. Depending on the fitness facility, email and text reminders for appointments can be appropriate if done through a business email or contact number. The personal trainer needs to be careful about sending personal information regarding the client through these avenues. Additionally, keeping an updated newsletter or website can be a means of communicating mass information to several clients; however, some clients may not use these sources as a general rule.

Verbal and nonverbal communication

Communication throughout the exercise session is both verbal and nonverbal. The personal trainer should give verbal instructions and encouragement to the client while also realizing that her body language will impact the client as well. It is important to make eye contact with the client and speak kindly and confidently to him so he understands that his personal trainer views his time and effort as important. The personal trainer should maintain a professional appearance at all times, maintaining a pleasant facial expression and keeping her attention focused on the client throughout the session.

Active listening

Active listening means that the personal trainer is listening to what the client has to say, looking at the client while she speaks, and asking questions at appropriate times to be sure of what the client means. Examples of active listening would be making eye contact with the client, jotting down notes regarding what the client is saying, ensuring he understands the client's request ("So what I understand you to mean is…"), and making any necessary changes to the workout routine based on the client's feedback.

Interference with client faithfulness to exercise programming

There are many things that can interfere with client faithfulness to an exercise program. If there is extra stress in a client's personal life, he may be less inclined to follow through with appointments. Work schedule and finances can also cause unfaithfulness to exercise. Falling back into poor nutritional habits and subsequently using the guilt associated with it to cause him to cancel training times is not uncommon. If a client feels that the personal trainer is not an effective communicator, or is not listening to him, he may express reluctance in moving forward with more sessions. Sometimes clients may fear not getting the results they want to see for themselves, may not manage their time wisely, or may not understand how to implement changes at home that will help them in their training sessions. It is the trainer's job to help coach clients through these issues.

Influencing a client avoid detrimental behaviors

A personal trainer can help a client avoid many of the pitfalls associated with outside stressors or relapses into previous poor habits by creating an "open door policy." The trainer can encourage honesty from the client while offering encouragement and constructive advice for avoiding common pitfalls. Providing compassionate accountability is very necessary for clients who may be more prone to fall back into sedentary habits.

Professional Conduct, Safety, and Risk Management

Code of Ethics

A code of ethics represents some basic guidelines for behavior that members of a given profession adhere to. All major professions maintain ethical guidelines and some manner of compliance in order to ensure the quality of practitioners in that field and to keep the profession in good repute among the general public. This helps all members of the profession deliver the best services to its clients.

The ACE Code of Ethics is as follows:

As an ACE-certified Professional, I am guided by the American Council on Exercise's principles of professional conduct whether I am working with clients, the public or other health and fitness professionals. I promise to:

- Provide safe and effective instruction.
- Provide equal and fair treatment to all clients.
- Stay up-to-date on the latest health and fitness research and understand its practical application.
- Maintain current CPR and AED certificates and knowledge of first-aid services.
- Comply with all applicable business, employment and intellectual property laws.
- Uphold and enhance public appreciation and trust for the health and fitness industry.
- Maintain the confidentiality of all client information.
- Refer clients to more qualified health or medical professionals when appropriate.
- Establish and maintain clear professional boundaries.

Professional Practices and Disciplinary Procedures

The professional practices and disciplinary procedures of the American Council on Exercise® (ACE) are intended to assist and inform certificants, candidates for certification and the public of the ACE Application and Certification Standards relative to professional conduct and disciplinary procedures. ACE may revoke or otherwise take action with regard to the application or certification of an individual in the case of:

- Ineligibility for certification.
- Irregularity in connection with any certification examination.
- Unauthorized possession, use, access, or distribution of certification examinations, score reports, trademarks, logos, written materials, answer

sheets, certificates, certificant or applicant files, or other confidential or proprietary ACE documents or materials (registered or otherwise).
- Material misrepresentation or fraud in any statement to ACE or to the public, including but not limited to statements made to assist the applicant, certificant, or another to apply for, obtain, or retain certification.
- Any physical, mental, or emotional condition of either temporary or permanent nature, including, but not limited to, substance abuse, which impairs or has the potential to impair competent and objective professional performance.
- Negligent and/or intentional misconduct in professional work, including, but not limited to, physical or emotional abuse, disregard for safety, or the unauthorized release of confidential information.
- The timely conviction, plea of guilty, or plea of nolo contendere in connection with a felony or misdemeanor, which is directly related to public health and/or fitness instruction or education, which impairs competent and objective professional performance. These include, but are not limited to, rape, sexual abuse of a client, actual or threatened use of a weapon of violence, the prohibited sale, distribution, or possession with intent to distribute, of a controlled substance.
- Failure to meet the requirements for certification or recertification.

ACE has developed a three-tiered disciplinary process of review, hearing and appeals to ensure fair and unbiased examination of alleged violation(s) of the Application and Certification Standards in order to (1) determine the merit of allegations; and (2) impose appropriate sanctions as necessary to protect the public and the integrity of the certification process.

Stratifying client risk and obtaining medical clearance to minimize negligence

Negligence is defined as the breach of the duty of care between a professional and a client. If a personal trainer doesn't take time to stratify client risk and obtain medical clearance if indicated, she will be seen as negligent should anything happen to the client during the course of exercise programming. The personal trainer is obligated to do everything in her power to ensure the client is exercising in a safe environment with minimal risk to health and well-being; stratifying client risk and obtaining medical clearance meets this professional requirement.

Levels of risk stratification

The Health History Questionnaire enables clients to see specifically which risk factors affect them. For instance, the following risk factors could indicate coronary artery disease: hypertension, family history, high cholesterol, cigarette smoking, impaired fasting glucose, obesity, sedentary lifestyle. Additionally, risk factors can also be assessed during the exercise session. The following risk factors could indicate pulmonary, metabolic, or cardiovascular disease: pain or tension in chest, neck, jaws, arms, or other areas; dizziness; shortness of breath; orthopnea or nightly dyspnea; palpitations; ankle edema; known heart murmur; intermittent claudication; unusual fatigue or shortness of breath during normal activities. Clients can be stratified as low, moderate, or high risk based upon the aforementioned symptoms.

Medical clearance requirements

If a client answers yes to one or more questions indicating cardiovascular or metabolic or pulmonary disease and has a history of chronic disease, medical clearance is necessary to begin treatment through exercise. If a client answers yes to one or more of these questions, the personal trainer should take into account the health history as it is described by the client and should use his best judgment in recommending medical clearance or not. Generally, if the client was just barely placed in the moderate-risk category, but could be in the high-risk category very soon, medical clearance might be a good idea. Additionally, if the client responds poorly in the exercise testing, especially if she is unable to catch her breath or experiences heart palpitations, medical clearance is necessary.

Supervision for individuals who received medical clearance

Clients who have received medical clearance for exercise should be monitored continually during the exercise session. Additionally, they need to indicate how hard they feel they are working according to the RPE scale. These clients should never be left alone to exercise until they have come to a point where their risk factors are decreasing or it is deemed that they can exercise safely by themselves.

CPR and AED

A personal trainer should maintain a current CPR/AED certification at all times. If a client becomes unconscious or stops breathing at any time, CPR protocol should be initiated. AED protocol should be initiated as necessary if there is more than one person at hand in a situation where a client collapses. If a personal trainer does not maintain a current CPR/AED certification, she could be held liable for practicing without a license.

Emergency procedures clearly delineated for the client

The personal trainer should make clear to the client proper procedure in case of emergencies. For instance, in case of a fire or inclement weather, the client should know where the exits are or where to seek adequate shelter. Whenever the fitness facility updates its procedures, it is the personal trainer's responsibility to ensure the client knows what to do. Additionally, the personal trainer should have on file permission from the client to call emergency services or a medical practitioner if appropriate.

Basic first-aid procedures

Exercise intolerance

If a client is experiencing exercise intolerance, a cooldown should be initiated immediately to bring the client's heart rate back down to resting levels. The client needs to drink adequate amounts of water to maintain hydration. The client should continue moving as necessary until heart rate returns to normal. If the client feels dizzy or overheated, he can sit down, but lying down is contraindicated. The client should be given some cool water, and a cold towel or compress should be applied to his neck to reduce body temperature. If the client is having trouble breathing due to chest pains, medical personnel should be contacted as it may be exercise-induced angina.

Exercise-related injury

If the client has an exercise-related injury, the client should be put in a sitting position and RICE (rest, ice, compression, elevation) should be followed for the injured area as needed. A medical practitioner should be immediately called. This information should be kept on file prior to any exercise sessions taking place so it can be accessed in the event of an emergency. The personal trainer should also have on file a client's permission to call emergency services in the event of an emergency if it's deemed necessary.

Client safety in the fitness facility

Client safety can be ensured by having them engage in exercises that correspond to their current fitness level. Clients should also be taught how to correctly handle resistance machines and free weights to avoid personal injury. They should also be made aware of facility rules regarding flow of traffic inside the facility, appropriate cardiovascular machine usage, and age requirements for using equipment. Clients should never use a machine they do not know how to use; this can be remedied by the personal trainer giving a comprehensive education on machine usage.

Injuries

There are several injuries that can be common complaints of clients, and it is beneficial for personal trainers to know how to work around them during an exercise session. Shin splints are characterized by pain along the outside of the leg starting right below the knee. A sprain is pain in the joint where a ligament has been overstretched. A strain is characterized by muscle fibers tearing because of being overstretched. Bursitis is inflammation of the bursa sacs. Tendonitis is inflammation or irritation of a tendon. A fracture is a break in a bone. Patello-femoral pain syndrome is localized pain in front of the knee. Low back pain is localized pain across the lower back in the lumbar spine and pelvis. Plantar fasciitis is inflammation of the fascia on the bottom of the foot and often results in heel pain and tenderness.

If shin splints, sprain, or strain occur during the course of exercise, ice should be applied immediately and the ankle or other joint elevated. The client should be encouraged to wrap the area in a compression sleeve and visit a medical professional. If a fracture occurs, medical help should be sought immediately. A client with bursitis and tendonitis should engage in non–weight-bearing cardiovascular activities, and resistance activities should utilize resistance bands. If a client has patello-femoral pain syndrome, medical clearance should be given prior to exercise, and non–weight-bearing cardiovascular activity should be the focus. Resistance activities should be focused around machine weights. For low back pain and plantar fasciitis, the warm-up and stretch segments should be extended, and myofascial release techniques should be utilized.

Liability during emergency procedures

When an emergency situation happens and the client is directly under the personal trainer's supervision, the personal trainer is held liable for what happens to the client. The personal trainer is responsible for the client's safety while performing exercise, and if an emergency occurs within the fitness facility, the trainer must do her best to ensure the client's safety. The trainer must be up-to-date on fitness emergency procedures.

Management and first-aid during exercise

Common cardiovascular complications
If a cardiovascular event happens during an exercise session, the personal trainer needs to be aware of signs and symptoms that indicate it. The signs and symptoms are as follows: chest pain (or in head, neck, jaw, or arms), heart palpitations, hyperventilation, syncope, dyspnea, unusual shortness of breath during activities that typically do not bother the client, client's inability to speak. If any of these signs are present, the client may be suffering from exercise-induced angina, tachycardia, or asthma attack. Once exercise is ceased, if the symptoms do not go away, medical personnel should be called immediately. If the symptoms do go away, the client needs to seek medical attention prior to resuming exercise at the next session.

Common metabolic abnormalities
If a client is experiencing a metabolic abnormality during exercise, such as hypo- or hyperglycemia, the trainer should be aware of signs that indicate it. Signs indicating metabolic abnormalities are as follows: fainting, syncope, pale face, blurred vision, dry mouth, excessive sweating. For clients with known metabolic abnormalities, it is recommended for them to bring something to eat or drink in case of emergency.

Open wound

If a client has a wound that begins to bleed during an exercise session, the personal trainer should retrieve the first aid kit from the fitness facility. The client should be instructed to wash the wound with soap and water. The personal trainer should provide antiseptic and a band aid, and if necessary, help apply dressing. If the trainer needs to apply dressing, she should wear safety gloves that are included in the first aid kit.

Complications with musculoskeletal injuries

If the pain does not interfere with the client's ability to express himself clearly, the personal trainer should ask the client what the pain feels like (i.e., sharp pain or dull pain); if the injury occurs in one of the limbs, the personal trainer needs to apply the RICE method where appropriate. If the injury is to the head, neck, or spine, the personal trainer needs to initiate emergency or first aid procedures depending on whether first aid staff are available at the fitness center. The trainer should never attempt to move the client in this situation. Additionally, in order to remain within the accepted scope of practice, the personal trainer should ask the client to seek medical attention to treat the injury.

Complications of cardiovascular or pulmonary issues

If complications arise during an exercise session that could indicate cardiovascular or pulmonary issues, the client needs to first lower the intensity of the exercise, assess heart rate to ensure it is coming down from where it was, and ask the client questions about how she is feeling to assess whether she can talk. If the client can't talk, the intensity of the exercise needs to be lowered further. If heart rate remains erratic, or complications continue, the client needs to initiate cooldown. After cooldown, the trainer should stay with the client until heart rate is within 10 or fewer beats above the resting heart rate. Additionally, the client needs to drink some water.

Complications due to metabolic syndromes

If complications due to metabolic syndrome arise during an exercise session, the personal trainer needs to follow protocol similar to when complications are due to cardiovascular or pulmonary issues. The personal trainer must keep in mind that the client should never be left alone during this time. If reducing intensity of the workout helps the client reduce symptoms of complications, the trainer and client assess together that the client is able to continue the session, and no absolute contraindications are present, then the client can continue the session at the reduced intensity.

Ongoing evaluation of exercise equipment

A fitness center should maintain its equipment according to manufacturer guidelines. Manufacturer handbooks should be kept on file and easily accessible. Machines should be cleaned between client use throughout the day, and clients should be encouraged and instructed on how to clean the machines as they finish with them. All equipment should be checked daily to ensure it is in proper working order.

Ensuring safety policies and procedures are well-known among clients

A fitness center should have all exits clearly marked. Procedures for emergency situations (fire, inclement weather, etc.) should be clearly posted. Additionally, the personal trainer should go through the procedures with clients to ensure understanding. Clients should be trained on equipment usage to avoid injury and to have confidence in using the fitness center on their own.

The personal trainer can assess client understanding of emergency procedures in a variety of ways. The trainer can verbally go through the steps of emergency response with the client. Additionally, he can practice the procedures with the client and allow time for questions regarding them. Ongoing assessment should occur. The trainer needs to be aware that it is his shared responsibility with the facility to ensure that the client understands all emergency procedures. The client should regularly practice all procedures.

If clients and staff don't properly understand how to act in an emergency situation, injuries can happen and unsafe behaviors can occur. Additionally, the fitness center can be held liable for any injuries or an unsafe situation that arises due to negligence. Procedures need to be put in place to safeguard the general well-being of the client/customer; if this is neglected, it becomes an issue of liability for the facility. If something were to happen to a client during an emergency that could have been avoided with proper training for the emergency situation, the fitness facility bears responsibility for that injury.

Keeping up-to-date with current research

Current research allows personal trainers to maintain understanding of changes in their field of practice and the scientific research that underlies those changes. This becomes important because trainers need to understand the physiology of their practice and the reason for changes that need to occur. Understanding this information allows them to synthesize it and explain it to their clients in a way that makes sense, which ultimately helps maintain motivation and adherence to their exercise program because they understand why they are performing the specified activities.

Negligence

Personal trainers can be tempted to practice outside of the scope of their certification, especially when clients ask for their advice on topics better suited to physical therapy or a rehabilitation specialist. It can also be tempting at the end of a long day for a personal trainer to become distracted and not pay attention to the client, which can increase the possibility of injury. Also, when the trainer and client become very familiar with each other, they may be more likely to chat freely during the session. This sometimes encourages the personal trainer to not pay attention to technique as diligently as he might otherwise have.

Risk management techniques to minimize liability

Personal trainers must take care to keep their eyes and ears open at all times for the safety of their clients. Cell phones and anything else that would be distracting to the trainer should be put away. Sessions should be properly documented so if any questions arise, they can be answered in a timely way. Where necessary, the trainer should keep medical personnel up-to-date with pertinent information regarding the client. Clients should not be allowed to exercise on equipment that exceeds their current abilities, and trainers should not promise to help with training details that lie outside their scope of practice.

Equipment maintenance and client safety

Equipment should be checked weekly to ensure it remains in proper working order. If it isn't working properly, a sign should be put in clear view that puts the machine out of commission until maintenance is able to fix the issue. If equipment is broken, the client may be injured while trying to operate it.

Practice Test

Practice Questions

1. The joint movement that results in an increase of the joint angle is called
    a. Abduction
    b. Adduction
    c. Extension
    d. Flexion

2. Which of these muscles is not part of the Rotator cuff?
    a. Supraspinatus
    b. Infraspinatus
    c. Teres minor
    d. Teres major

3. Which of the following should be considered a life-threatening medical emergency?
    a. Anterior cruciate ligament tear
    b. A dislocation of the cervical spinal cord
    c. An Achilles' tendon rupture
    d. A hip fracture in an elderly individual

4. Which of the following can cause pain in the lumbar area?
    a. Strain of the tibialis anterior muscle
    b. Strain of the longissimus thoracis muscle
    c. Strain of the gastrocnemius muscle
    d. Strain of the sternocleidomastoid muscle

5. When working with a trainer, an individual lifts a 10-pound weight straight over her head through a distance of 2.5 feet. How much linear work has been generated?
    a. 4 pound-feet
    b. 7.5 pound-feet
    c. 25 pound-feet
    d. 50 pound-feet

6. For average groups of people represented below, which order represents the lowest resting heart rate to the highest resting heart rate?
    a. Men, women, children, elderly individuals
    b. Children, women, elderly individuals, men
    c. Elderly individuals, women, men, children
    d. Elderly individuals, men, women, children

7. The body recruits type I muscle fibers for activities of
    a. long duration and low intensity
    b. long duration and high intensity
    c. short duration and high intensity
    d. none of the above

8. All of the following classes of nutrients provide sources of energy EXCEPT
    a. proteins
    b. vitamins
    c. fats
    d. carbohydrates

9. A nonathlete who weighs 80 kg would require _____ grams per day of protein.
    a. 50 grams
    b. 80 grams
    c. 64 grams
    d. 100 grams

10. A deficiency of which vitamin can lead to difficulty seeing at night and an increased susceptibility to infections?
    a. vitamin B1
    b. vitamin B3
    c. vitamin E
    d. vitamin A

11. You are exercising outdoors and become concerned that your client may be dehydrated. At what point would her condition be considered a medical emergency?
    a. When she complains that her leg muscles are cramping
    b. When she seems to be confused and doesn't know where she is
    c. When she becomes dizzy and light-headed
    d. When she begins complaining of a headache

12. What food information is NOT present on a food label?
    a. amount of protein in a serving
    b. amount of cholesterol in a serving
    c. amount of calories in a serving
    d. amount of caffeine in a serving

13. When meeting with a client for the first time, all of the following can be helpful comments to make to a client EXCEPT
    a. "How would you like this work to help you?"
    b. "Can you tell me about your daily routine?"
    c. "What heath problems do you have?"
    d. "Do you think you have clinical depression?"

14. A client in the precontemplation stage of behavior might think to himself:
    a. "I just can't lose weight."
    b. "I have a plan to lose weight."
    c. "I am really thinking about how to lose weight."
    d. "I am so proud I lost weight!"

15. An example of a substitution behavioral change that you might suggest to a client is
    a. "Call your best friend to walk with you every day."
    b. "Take the stairs instead of the elevator at work."
    c. "If you reach this goal we set up, you can have a reward of your choosing."
    d. "Put your running shoes right by your bed so you are motivated to run first thing in the morning."

16. Your client is in the maintenance stage of behavior and is exercising regularly. One day she cancels her appointments with you, claiming she has too much to do at work. If she abandons her exercise routine completely, it is called a
    a. lapse
    b. self-change
    c. relapse
    d. self-challenge

17. All of the following can help the client-trainer relationship EXCEPT
    a. Accepting your client for what she is able to do, even if others her age are able to do more
    b. Asking your client about his week
    c. Answering a text or phone call during a session
    d. Keeping information between the two of you confidential

18. An example of active listening is
    a. "Why didn't you do this exercise this week?"
    b. "Great job with your exercises this week!"
    c. "How did your big project at work turn out?"
    d. "So you are saying that you didn't understand how this exercise was supposed to feel?"

19. The interactive tool that can lead to change by creating an equal partnership between the client and the trainer is called
    a. Motivational interviewing
    b. Generative moments
    c. Appreciative inquiry
    d. Change talk

20. Goals that a trainer helps a client set should be all of the following EXCEPT
    a. Time-limited
    b. Action-based
    c. Broadly defined
    d. Measurable

21. Active listening, building rapport, and showing understanding of a client's situation are all components of
    a. Nonverbal communication
    b. Intrinsic motivation
    c. Extrinsic motivation
    d. Client-centered techniques

22. As a prelude to creating a personal training package for a client, a trainer should obtain all of the following EXCEPT
    a. Approval and signature of a physician
    b. Informed consent from the client
    c. Permission to post the client's photo on the trainer's Web site
    d. Health history of the client

23. A number of atherosclerotic cardiovascular disease risk factors exist. A client who has which of the following would be considered to have a positive risk factor for hypertension?
    a. Systolic blood pressure ≥ 140 mm Hg on two separate occasions
    b. Diastolic blood pressure ≥75 mm Hg on two separate occasions
    c. Systolic blood pressure ≥ 140 mm Hg and diastolic blood pressure ≥ 100 mm Hg on one occasion
    d. Having taken an antihypertensive medication in the past

24. Shortness of breath at rest is called
    a. Ischemia
    b. Dyspnea
    c. Syncope
    d. Orthopnea

25. All of the following are true of intermittent claudication EXCEPT
    a. People with diabetes have a greater risk of having intermittent claudication.
    b. Intermittent claudication does not usually occur when a client stands or sits.
    c. Intermittent claudication usually goes away within 10 minutes of stopping an exercise.
    d. Symptoms associated with intermittent claudication are reproducible.

26. Which of the following pulses is not commonly used to determine an individual's heart rate?
    a. Carotid
    b. Brachial
    c. Radial
    d. Popliteal

27. Normal systolic and diastolic blood pressure measurements (in mm Hg) include which of the following?
    a. Systolic 110, diastolic 75
    b. Systolic 130, diastolic 70
    c. Systolic 140, diastolic 85
    d. Systolic 110, diastolic 85

28. An individual weighs 80 kg and is 1.75 meters tall. What range does his BMI fall into?
    a. Normal
    b. Overweight
    c. Obese class I
    d. Obese class II

29. The Rockport is a field test that involves
    a. Running continuously for 1.5 miles
    b. Walking intermittently for 2 miles
    c. Stepping up and down continuously for 3 minutes
    d. Walking as fast as possible for 1 mile

30. An individual's flexibility can be assessed by which of the following?
    a. A one-repetition bench press
    b. A sit-and-reach test
    c. A push-up test
    d. A curl-up test

31. The hip joint is what type of joint?
    a. Ball-and-socket joint
    b. Hinge joint
    c. Cartilaginous joint
    d. Pivot joint

32. The primary function of the respiratory system is
    a. Delivering nutrients to tissues in the body
    b. Regulating the body's pH level
    c. Facilitating the exchange of oxygen and carbon dioxide
    d. Maintaining fluid volume to prevent dehydration

33. The type of stretching that requires assistance from a personal trainer is called
    a. Active stretching
    b. Passive stretching
    c. Ballistic stretching
    d. Static stretching

34. All of the following are benefits of increased flexibility EXCEPT
    a. Improved circulation
    b. Increased range of motion
    c. Improved coordination
    d. Increased chance of muscle injury

35. The condition that involves rapid breakdown of muscle tissue due to too much exercise, which can potentially result in kidney failure, is called
    a. Myoglobinuria
    b. Rhabdomyolysis
    c. Dialysis
    d. Proteinuria

36. Benefits of nonlinear periodized training programs include all of the following EXCEPT
    a. Using a progressive increase in the workout intensity
    b. Allowing for variation in the workout intensity
    c. Having a "power" training day
    d. Training both power and strength of muscles within one week

37. What is the approximate target heart rate for a 50-year-old man in beats per minute (bpm)?
    a. 75 to 120
    b. 85 to 110
    c. 95 to 140
    d. 120 to 160

38. An effective cardiorespiratory training program session should include all of these basic components EXCEPT
    a. Power phase
    b. Cool-down phase
    c. Warm-up phase
    d. Endurance phase

39. The "talk test" refers to
    a. The practice of speaking with your client before a training session to check in with the client
    b. The practice of talking with your client during the cool-down phase to see how the session felt.
    c. The ability of an individual while exercising to talk or respond to a trainer's questions without gasping for breath.
    d. The comfort level of a client to let a trainer know when an exercise is too hard.

40. Individuals with osteoporosis
    a. Should not do flexibility training exercises
    b. Should avoid twisting or flexing of the spine
    c. Should not worry about proper breathing techniques
    d. Are not more likely to develop fractures

41. Which of the following inhibits a person's joint flexibility?
    a. Having cold muscles
    b. Being a woman
    c. Having more relaxed muscles
    d. Having a more physically active lifestyle

42. Older adults should engage in an aerobic exercise program that provides which of the following?
    a. 25 minutes, 3 days a week of mild intensity aerobic activity
    b. 30 minutes, 3 days a week of moderate intensity aerobic activity
    c. 20 minutes, 5 days a week of vigorous intensity aerobic activity
    d. 30 minutes, 5 days a week of moderate intensity aerobic activity

43. Which of the following conditions is an absolute contraindication for exercising during pregnancy?
    a. Poorly controlled seizure disorder
    b. Ruptured membranes
    c. Heavy smoker
    d. Poorly controlled hypertension

44. Common complications of diabetes include all of the following EXCEPT
    a. Kidney problems
    b. Vision problems
    c. Hearing problems
    d. Peripheral nerve problems

45. How much weight loss is appropriate for an obese individual with a BMI greater than 30?
    a. 1 kg a week
    b. 2 kg a week
    c. 3 kg a week
    d. 4 kg a week

46. Which of the following is not covered when obtaining informed consent from a client?
    a. Benefits that the client should expect to gain
    b. Risks and discomfort that may be associated with the training program
    c. Purpose of the training program
    d. How much the training program will cost

47. The end of a bone is called the
    a. Epiphysis
    b. Periosteum
    c. Endosteum
    d. Diaphysis

48. All are true of a synovial joint EXCEPT
    a. The synovial cavity is filled with synovial fluid.
    b. A synovial joint can flex and extend.
    c. A synovial joint may be supported by ligaments.
    d. A synovial joint never contains any other structures inside of it.

49. Leg raises are an example of
    a. Hip extension
    b. Knee flexion
    c. Hip flexion
    d. Hip abduction

50. Which function does the autonomic nervous system NOT regulate?
    a. Digestion
    b. Breathing
    c. Running
    d. Secretion of hormones

Answer Key and Explanations

1. C: When a joint is extended, the angle of the joint is increased. Flexion is the opposite of extension, and causes the joint angle to decrease. Abduction refers to movement that is directed away from the midline of the body. The opposite of abduction is adduction. Adduction describes movements that are made toward the midline of the body.

2. D: The Supraspinatus is an abductor of the arm. The Infraspinatus and Teres minor are both external rotators. The Subscapularis is the missing muscle of the rotator cuff.

3. B: Any trauma to the neck (or cervical spine) should be considered a medical emergency. When the cervical vertebrae are dislocated or fractured, the spinal column can become unstable. This can potentially lead to paralysis or death. While an Achilles' tendon rupture or anterior cruciate ligament tear is a serious leg/knee injury, respectively, and may be career ending for athletes, either one is not life threatening. A hip fracture or a fracture of the neck of the femur can cause permanent disability, especially in the elderly. However, these are also not usually life threatening.

4. B: The longissimus thoracis muscle is located in the posterior lumbar region. It is part of the erector spinae group. These muscles help maintain posture and provide stability to the spine. Lumbar pain, also called low back pain, is one of the most common causes of disability. About 60 to 80% of the general population will experience it at some point in their lives. Determining the specific cause of lumbar pain may be difficult, but muscle strain, an intervertebral herniated disc, and joint inflammation can all cause lumbar pain. The other muscles are not located in the lumbar region. The sternocleidomastoid muscle is located in the cervical region. Strain to this muscle occurs with "whiplash" injuries. The tibialis anterior muscle is located on the anterior and lateral part of the lower leg. The gastrocnemius muscle is located on the posterior part of the lower leg.

5. C: Multiplying the force times the distance through which the force travels will result in the linear work generated. Ten times 2.5 equals 25.

6. D: Heart rate is the number of times that the heart beats per minute and can be measured by taking a pulse. Average people have a resting heart rate of 60 to 80 beats per minute (bpm). The elderly have a lower resting heart rate than adult men and women. Men have a resting heart rate that is about 10 bpm lower than that of adult women. Children have resting heart rates that are higher than

those of adults. When comparing fit to unfit individuals, fit individuals have a lower resting heart rate.

7. A: The body has two types of muscle fibers: type I and type II. Together, these muscle fibers can do all types of tasks. However, the body recruits each type during different activities or specific times of an activity, depending on the type and duration of motion required. Type I muscle fibers, also called slow-twitch fibers, are used for activities of long duration and low intensity, such as those involving endurance. In contrast, type II muscle fibers are employed for high-speed, high-power tasks. These muscle fibers are capable of generating force more quickly than type I muscle fibers.

8. B: Carbon is critical for the energy production process. Proteins, fats, and carbohydrates—which are all sources of carbon—contribute to a number of functions in the body. They help provide energy so that muscles, nerves, and metabolic processes work normally. Energy is measured in calories (cal) or kilocalories (kcal). When individuals exercise, they can "burn" energy more quickly. Vitamins and minerals are critical for providing essential nutrients that the body needs to maintain normal function; however, they are not a source of energy.

9. C: The average person's daily requirement for protein is 0.8 g/kg. In other words, multiplying 0.8 by the person's weight in kilograms will give the daily amount of protein in grams needed. For this individual, that would be 80×0.8 = 64 grams. Athletes require more protein each day—about 1.2 to 2 g/kg of body weight. If this individual were an athlete, he or she would require between 96 and 160 grams of protein per day. In addition to these specific recommendations, it is also recommended that protein account for about 12 to 15% of the total calories a person eats each day.

10. D: Vitamin A, known as retinol, is found in foods such as fish liver oils, butter, and egg yolks. It is critical for red blood cell and embryo development and normal functioning of the eyes, the immune system, and the skin. Vitamin B_1 is also called thiamin. A deficiency of this vitamin can lead to beriberi. Symptoms of beriberi can include cardiovascular problems, peripheral neuropathy, and cognitive and psychiatric problems. Vitamin B_3 is also known as niacin; a deficiency of this vitamin can cause a disease called pellagra. Pellagra can cause a skin rash, gastrointestinal symptoms, or cognitive difficulties. If untreated, it can also lead to death. Vitamin E is an antioxidant that augments the immune system. It can help prevent cell membranes from being destroyed by harmful free radicals.

11. B: Dehydration, heat exhaustion, and heat stroke are conditions that are best avoided by encouraging clients to drink either water or sports drinks often. When individuals wait until they feel thirsty to drink, they may already have

lost 1 to 2 liters of fluid. A dehydrated individual may feel less energetic and begin to develop muscle cramps. If not treated, an individual can develop heat exhaustion, which may be manifested by headaches and feelings of nausea. If heat exhaustion isn't treated, an individual may suffer from heat stroke. During heat stroke, an individual's body temperature increases, and he or she may become confused or lose consciousness. This is a medical emergency. The patient needs to have her body temperature lowered as quickly as possible.

12. D: Labeling on food packages is helpful in determining a number of characteristics of a food, including the ingredients, serving size, and nutrients present in the food. Food label information is based on a 2,000 calorie diet. It provides the percent daily value for the amount of fats, cholesterol, sodium, potassium, carbohydrates, and protein present in a serving size. While caffeine will be listed as an ingredient if it is present in the food, the specific amount of caffeine will not be listed.

13. D: It is important to remember that coaching is not therapy or mental health counseling. Personal trainers should never diagnose current psychiatric problems. However, it is important to ask a person about their past history— medical and otherwise—so that your sessions can be appropriate and productive. Knowing about a person's daily routine will tell you how active he or she usually is. Asking, "How would you like this work to help you?" can elicit a specific goal that the two of you can work toward.

14. A: There are five stages of behavioral change. Listed in order of unwilling to change to readiness to change, they are precontemplation, contemplation, preparation, action, and maintenance. People in precontemplation often say, "I can't" or "I won't" about being able to change. People in the contemplation stage often say, "I just may change" or "I'm thinking about it." People in the preparation stage have actively decided to take action at some point soon. In the action stage, a person has decided to implement a consistent change, but has been implementing the new behavior for less than six months. If a person has consistently implemented a change for more than six months, he or she is in the maintenance stage.

15. B: There are a number of strategies trainers can employ in order to effect behavior change in a client. Substitution or counterconditioning involves substituting healthy behaviors for unhealthy behaviors. Answer A is an example of social support. Answer C is an example of a reward or reinforcement system. Answer D is an example of environmental control, which is a cue that can precipitate healthy behavior.

16. C: A relapse is when a person stops their positive behavior and, as a result, loses the positive benefits he or she had gained. Many conditions can lead to relapse; work pressures, boredom, and increased travel are only a few.

Although similar, a lapse is a temporary stop in positive behavior. Had this client returned after a week or two, her exercise routine would have lapsed, but she would have likely maintained or quickly regained the positive benefits.

17. C: A number of factors can help facilitate a beneficial working relationship between a client and a trainer. These can include being present in the moment, maintaining confidentiality, being interested in your client's life, giving helpful feedback, and treating your client in a positive way. Along those lines, it is important to accept clients at the level they are currently at, rather than comparing them to others.

18. D: Active listening is a technique than enhances communication. It involves conveying what the client says back to the client, so that the individual feels they are being heard and understood. The client tells you how he or she feels or what he or she thinks, and you repeat or paraphrase it back to the individual. This technique provides the opportunity for clarification in the event that the client actually meant something else. When actively listening, it is helpful to let the other speak without interruption and to maintain eye contact and focus on the client.

19. A: Motivational interviewing is based on the idea that change occurs when there is an equal partnership between the client and trainer. While you are a training expert, your client is an expert is his or her own life. Motivational interviewing is used in a client-centered relationship. Generative moments are powerful or negative events that have happened to a client that can spur him or her to change. Appreciative inquiry is a technique in which the trainer asks positive and powerful questions to help the client visualize potential possibilities. Change talk involves language spoken by a client about his or her desire and ability to change their behavior.

20. C: Goals that are most helpful are those that are specific, very well defined, able to be measured, realistic, and have a time constraint on them. The actions a client needs to take should be specifically defined. For example, a goal may be that a client will walk on his treadmill at a pace of 3 mph for 30 minutes on Monday through Friday before going to work.

21. D: Client-centered techniques include asking open-ended questions, listening actively, and frequently clarifying what the client says. These can all contribute to building rapport and a strong relationship with a client. Nonverbal communication is that which is expressed and received via nonverbal cues, such as facial expressions, gestures, and the presence or absence of eye contact. Intrinsic motivation is the motivation for change that comes from within. For example, a person may want to lose weight to feel proud or to feel like he can achieve a goal. When people are extrinsically motivated, they are motivated to

achieve a goal because of an external factor. For example, someone might want to lose weight to fit into a wedding dress.

22. C: While you should always obtain permission before posting a photo of a client on a Web site, that is not one of the critical initial pieces of information. If medical clearance is necessary, a signature and recommendations from your client's physician should be obtained. In addition, you will need to know your client's past and present medical and health issues to create an appropriate training plan. You will also need informed consent from your client, demonstrating that he or she understands the risk and benefits of undertaking a training program.

23. A: Hypertension is defined by the Seventh Report of the Joint National Committee on Prevention, Detection, Evaluation, and Treatment of High Blood Pressure as a systolic blood pressure of ≥ 140 mm Hg and a diastolic blood pressure of ≥ 90 mm Hg on two separate occasions. In addition, current use of an antihypertensive medication is considered to be a positive risk factor for hypertension.

24. B: A client with dyspnea will have shortness of breath while resting or only with mild exertion. It is not normal, and it can be a symptom of cardiac or pulmonary disease. Orthopnea is shortness of breath that occurs when one is lying down. It is relieved by sitting upright or standing. Ischemia occurs when there is a lack of blood flow and oxygen to the heart. This causes pain in the chest or pain that has radiated to the neck or arm. Syncope is a loss of consciousness that usually occurs when the brain does not receive enough oxygen.

25. C: When an individual has intermittent claudication, he or she will develop pain in a specific area with exercise due to inadequate blood flow to that specific muscle. This pain can be reproduced from day to day. It usually does not occur when a client is sitting or standing. People with coronary artery disease or diabetes are prone to developing intermittent claudication. However, once the exercise that precipitated the pain has stopped, the pain should go away within one to two minutes.

26. D: The popliteal artery, located behind the knee, can be difficult to palpate. The carotid pulse is felt by placing one's fingers lightly in the lower neck, along the medial aspect of the sternocleidomastoid muscle. The brachial pulse can be palpated between the triceps and biceps muscles on the anterior and medial aspect of the arm, near the elbow. The radial artery can be palpated on the anterior arm, near the wrist.

27. A: Normal blood pressure is classified as a systolic pressure of less than 120 mm Hg and a diastolic pressure of less than 80 mm Hg. If either the systolic or

diastolic pressures are elevated on multiple occasions, an individual's blood pressure is considered to be high.

28. B: BMI stands for body mass index, and it can be calculated by dividing an individual's weight by height squared. In this example, BMI = 80 kg / $(1.75 \text{ m})^2$. This results in a BMI of 26.1. BMI values fall into a range. The normal range is 18.5–24.9. The overweight range is 25–29.9. The obese class I range is 30–34.9. The obese class II range is 35–39.9.

29. D: The Rockport 1-mile walk test involves having a client walk as fast as he or she can for a distance of 1 mile. The individual must not run at all during this test. At the end of the test, the individual's pulse and heart rate are measured. The Queens College Step Test involves having an individual step up and down on a standardized step height continuously for 3 minutes and then measuring his or her pulse and heart rate after the 3 minutes.

30. B: A sit-and-reach test can measure the flexibility of an individual's lower back, hip, and hamstrings. A one-repetition bench press is used to assess muscular strength or muscle force. Both the push-up test and the curl-up test are used for measuring muscle endurance.

31. A: The hip joint as well as the shoulder joint can move in all directions. They are ball-and-socket joints. A hinge joint can only move in one plane, such as with knee flexion and extension. A cartilaginous joint is a strong joint that is very slightly movable, such as intervertebral joints. A pivot joint is a joint in one plane that permits rotation, such as the humeroradial joint.

32. C: The respiratory system involves the lungs and is where the exchange of oxygen for carbon dioxide occurs. The cardiovascular system, which involves the heart and blood vessels, is responsible for delivering oxygen and nutrients to all tissues in the body, regulating the body's pH level to prevent acidosis or alkalosis, and maintaining fluid volume to prevent dehydration.

33. B: In passive stretching, a client remains relaxed, allowing a trainer to stretch the client's muscles. Ballistic stretching, which involves a bouncing-like movement, can cause injury to muscles if not performed carefully. Static stretching involves movements that are deliberate and sustained. Active stretching involves stretching muscles throughout their range of motion.

34. D: Flexibility training has a number of benefits, including increased circulation, increased range of motion, improved muscle coordination, and decreased future chance of muscle injury.

35. B: Rhabdomyolysis, caused when an individual exercises too excessively, results in muscle damage and breakdown. These breakdown products, which

can include protein and myoglobin, then enter the bloodstream and have the potential to harm the kidneys. Kidney failure, and possibly death, can result. Symptoms of rhabdomyolysis can include muscle swelling, pain, and soreness. Myoglobinuria and proteinuria describe the conditions of having myoglobin and protein in the urine. However, they do necessarily reflect a cause. Dialysis is a treatment for kidney failure.

36. A: While a linear periodized training program involves having a progressive increase in the workout intensity over the course of a week, a nonlinear periodized training program involves variation of intensity over the course of a week. A weeklong nonlinear periodized training program can target both muscle strength and power. A "power" training day involving power sets can also be implemented. This type of program may be more conducive to individuals with scheduling conflicts.

37. C: To calculate an individual's target heart rate, first one needs to estimate the person's maximal heart rate. This is estimated by subtracting a person's age from 200. In this example, the person's maximal heart rate is 200 – 50 = 150. Using this number, the target heart rate can be calculated. The recommended target heart rate is between 64% (or 70%) and 94% of the maximal heart rate. This would be 150 × 0.64 = 96, and 150 × 0.94 = 141. So, the individual's target heart rate is estimated to be between about 95 and 140 bpm.

38. A: A training program needs to balance many different variables in order to be effective. A trainer needs to take a client's goals, daily routines, and preferences into account to create a routine that will be followed. Each training session should include a warm-up phase, a workout or endurance phase, and then a cool-down phase.

39. C: It is important that a training session not be too intense. The "talk test" is a simple way to get a handle on the intensity of the endurance or workout phase. A client should be able to talk or answer a trainer's questions without gasping for breath. Not being able to speak easily can indicate that the workout is too intense. Cardiovascular, muscular, and orthopedic injuries are more likely to occur when a workout is too intense.

40. B: Osteoporosis is a disease that involves a loss of bone mineral density. Osteopenia is a milder form of osteoporosis. Although people with osteoporosis are more susceptible to fractures due to the thinning of their bones, they are appropriate candidates for flexibility training programs. These programs can help improve posture and maintain the alignment of the spine. However, the program should avoid repetitive exercises that involve twisting or flexing of the spine. Everyone who participates in a flexibility training program should be taught proper breathing techniques.

41. A: A person's flexibility is reflected in his or her ability to move a joint, without pain, through a range of motion. In general, a number of factors are associated with increased flexibility. Younger people are more flexible than older individuals, and women are more flexible than men. Warmer, more relaxed muscles allow more joint flexibility than colder muscles. Individuals who are physically active are often more flexible than those who are not. In addition, the joint structure and health of the joint and its surrounding tissues affect an individual's flexibility.

42. D: If their medical issues allow it, individuals over the age of 65 can and should participate in exercise training programs. Aerobic, or cardiorespiratory, exercise can decrease morbidity and mortality rates in older individuals. The recommendations are for older individuals to engage in moderate intensity aerobic activity for 30 minutes, 5 days a week (150 minutes total), or to engage in vigorous intensity aerobic activity for 25 minutes, 3 days a week (75 minutes total). People can also do a combination of both.

43. B: Recent research supports a role for exercise programs during pregnancy. Goals of this type of program can include reducing low back pain and decreasing the risk for developing gestational diabetes. However, there do exist a number of absolute contraindications. Some of these include ruptured membranes, placenta previa after 26 weeks of gestation, premature labor, preeclampsia, and high-risk multiple gestation pregnancies. In contrast, relative contraindications include the individual being a heavy smoker, having poorly controlled diabetes or seizures, or having poorly controlled hypertension or hyperthyroid disease.

44. C: Diabetes can lead to kidney problems (nephropathy), trouble seeing (retinopathy), and decreased sensation of peripheral nerves (peripheral neuropathy). If these conditions are present, a trainer needs to adapt an exercise program accordingly. Some precautions that can be taken include keeping the blood pressure stable for retinopathy, avoiding exercise requiring high levels of coordination for peripheral neuropathy, or avoiding prolonged exercise for nephropathy.

45. A: People who are obese have a BMI greater than or equal to 30. These individuals are at a high risk of cardiac problems, certain types of cancers, and diabetes. Among other areas, training programs can focus on weight loss, promoting appetite control, and lowering the risk of associated medical issues. Weight loss should be gradual—not more than 1 kg per week. Aerobic training sessions five to seven times a week lasting 45–60 minutes per session may be helpful.

46. D: Obtaining informed consent at the beginning of a professional relationship can protect against potential later legal action. An informed consent document will discuss the reason for the training program, the risks or

discomfort that a client may experience, the responsibilities of the client, the benefits the client may reap, and it will offer the opportunity for a client to ask related questions. Fee structure and payments are not part of the informed consent.

47. A: When describing the anatomy of a bone, the epiphysis is the end of a bone and the diaphysis is the shaft of the bone. The periosteum is a membrane that covers the surface of a bone, except at the articular surfaces (joints). The endosteum is the lining of the bone marrow cavity and contains the cells necessary for new bone development.

48. D: A synovial joint is the most common type of joint found in the body and is made up of two articulating bones. Synovial fluid is present in the synovial cavity, which is lined by a synovial membrane. The joint is surrounded by a fibrous capsule, which can be supported by ligaments. Sometimes, a synovial joint may contain other structures, such as menisci (for example, in the knee) or fat pads. There are subtypes of synovial joints, including a hinge joint, ball-and-socket joint, and a pivot joint.

49. C: Leg raises are one type of exercise that works the hip flexor muscles. These muscles include the iliopsoas, rectus femoris, sartorius, and pectineus. Exercises for hip extension include squats or leg presses. Hip extensor muscles are the hamstrings and the gluteus maximus. Hip abduction exercises can be done with an exercise machine. Muscles involved with hip abduction include the tensor fascia latae, sartorius, and gluteus minimus and medius. Leg curl exercises involve knee flexion. Muscles involved with flexion of the knee are the hamstrings, gracilis, and popliteus.

50. C: The central nervous system is comprised of the brain and the spinal cord and is responsible for receiving, analyzing, interpreting, and acting on sensory information. The central nervous system is comprised of the peripheral and autonomic nervous systems. The autonomic nervous system is responsible for functions such as respiration, digestion, making hormones, and maintaining heart rate. The autonomic nervous system can be subdivided into the sympathetic nervous system, which is activated when the body is "stressed" and causes an increase in heart rate and respiratory rate and the parasympathetic nervous system, which is "in control" when the stressful stimulus is no longer present.

Secret Key #1 - Time is Your Greatest Enemy

Pace Yourself

Wear a watch. At the beginning of the test, check the time (or start a chronometer on your watch to count the minutes), and check the time after every few questions to make sure you are "on schedule."

If you are forced to speed up, do it efficiently. Usually one or more answer choices can be eliminated without too much difficulty. Above all, don't panic. Don't speed up and just begin guessing at random choices. By pacing yourself, and continually monitoring your progress against your watch, you will always know exactly how far ahead or behind you are with your available time. If you find that you are one minute behind on the test, don't skip one question without spending any time on it, just to catch back up. Take 15 fewer seconds on the next four questions, and after four questions you'll have caught back up. Once you catch back up, you can continue working each problem at your normal pace.

Furthermore, don't dwell on the problems that you were rushed on. If a problem was taking up too much time and you made a hurried guess, it must be difficult. The difficult questions are the ones you are most likely to miss anyway, so it isn't a big loss. It is better to end with more time than you need than to run out of time.

Lastly, sometimes it is beneficial to slow down if you are constantly getting ahead of time. You are always more likely to catch a careless mistake by working more slowly than quickly, and among very high-scoring test takers (those who are likely to have lots of time left over), careless errors affect the score more than mastery of material.

Secret Key #2 - Guessing is not Guesswork

You probably know that guessing is a good idea - unlike other standardized tests, there is no penalty for getting a wrong answer. Even if you have no idea about a question, you still have a 20-25% chance of getting it right.

Most test takers do not understand the impact that proper guessing can have on their score. Unless you score extremely high, guessing will significantly contribute to your final score.

Monkeys Take the Test

What most test takers don't realize is that to insure that 20-25% chance, you have to guess randomly. If you put 20 monkeys in a room to take this test, assuming they answered once per question and behaved themselves, on average they would get 20-25% of the questions correct. Put 20 test takers in the room, and the average will be much lower among guessed questions. Why?
  1. The test writers intentionally write deceptive answer choices that "look" right. A test taker has no idea about a question, so picks the "best looking" answer, which is often wrong. The monkey has no idea what looks good and what doesn't, so will consistently be lucky about 20-25% of the time.
  2. Test takers will eliminate answer choices from the guessing pool based on a hunch or intuition. Simple but correct answers often get excluded, leaving a 0% chance of being correct. The monkey has no clue, and often gets lucky with the best choice.

This is why the process of elimination endorsed by most test courses is flawed and detrimental to your performance- test takers don't guess, they make an ignorant stab in the dark that is usually worse than random.

$5 Challenge

Let me introduce one of the most valuable ideas of this course- the $5 challenge:

You only mark your "best guess" if you are willing to bet $5 on it.
You only eliminate choices from guessing if you are willing to bet $5 on it.

Why $5? Five dollars is an amount of money that is small yet not insignificant, and can really add up fast (20 questions could cost you $100). Likewise, each answer choice on one question of the test will have a small impact on your overall score, but it can really add up to a lot of points in the end.

The process of elimination IS valuable. The following shows your chance of guessing it right:

If you eliminate wrong answer choices until only this many remain:	Chance of getting it correct:
1	100%
2	50%
3	33%

However, if you accidentally eliminate the right answer or go on a hunch for an incorrect answer, your chances drop dramatically: to 0%. By guessing among all the answer choices, you are GUARANTEED to have a shot at the right answer.

That's why the $5 test is so valuable- if you give up the advantage and safety of a pure guess, it had better be worth the risk.

What we still haven't covered is how to be sure that whatever guess you make is truly random. Here's the easiest way:

Always pick the first answer choice among those remaining.

Such a technique means that you have decided, **before you see a single test question**, exactly how you are going to guess- and since the order of choices tells you nothing about which one is correct, this guessing technique is perfectly random.

This section is not meant to scare you away from making educated guesses or eliminating choices- you just need to define when a choice is worth eliminating. The $5 test, along with a pre-defined random guessing strategy, is the best way to make sure you reap all of the benefits of guessing.

Secret Key #3 - Practice Smarter, Not Harder

Many test takers delay the test preparation process because they dread the awful amounts of practice time they think necessary to succeed on the test. We have refined an effective method that will take you only a fraction of the time.

There are a number of "obstacles" in your way to succeed. Among these are answering questions, finishing in time, and mastering test-taking strategies. All must be executed on the day of the test at peak performance, or your score will suffer. The test is a mental marathon that has a large impact on your future.

Just like a marathon runner, it is important to work your way up to the full challenge. So first you just worry about questions, and then time, and finally strategy:

Success Strategy

1. Find a good source for practice tests.
2. If you are willing to make a larger time investment, consider using more than one study guide- often the different approaches of multiple authors will help you "get" difficult concepts.
3. Take a practice test with no time constraints, with all study helps "open book." Take your time with questions and focus on applying strategies.
4. Take a practice test with time constraints, with all guides "open book."
5. Take a final practice test with no open material and time limits
If you have time to take more practice tests, just repeat step 5. By gradually exposing yourself to the full rigors of the test environment, you will condition your mind to the stress of test day and maximize your success.

Secret Key #4 - Prepare, Don't Procrastinate

Let me state an obvious fact: if you take the test three times, you will get three different scores. This is due to the way you feel on test day, the level of preparedness you have, and, despite the test writers' claims to the contrary, some tests WILL be easier for you than others.

Since your future depends so much on your score, you should maximize your chances of success. In order to maximize the likelihood of success, you've got to prepare in advance. This means taking practice tests and spending time learning the information and test taking strategies you will need to succeed.

Never take the test as a "practice" test, expecting that you can just take it again if you need to. Feel free to take sample tests on your own, but when you go to take the official test, be prepared, be focused, and do your best the first time!

Secret Key #5 - Test Yourself

Everyone knows that time is money. There is no need to spend too much of your time or too little of your time preparing for the test. You should only spend as much of your precious time preparing as is necessary for you to get the score you need.

Once you have taken a practice test under real conditions of time constraints, then you will know if you are ready for the test or not.

If you have scored extremely high the first time that you take the practice test, then there is not much point in spending countless hours studying. You are already there.

Benchmark your abilities by retaking practice tests and seeing how much you have improved. Once you score high enough to guarantee success, then you are ready.

If you have scored well below where you need, then knuckle down and begin studying in earnest. Check your improvement regularly through the use of practice tests under real conditions. Above all, don't worry, panic, or give up. The key is perseverance!

Then, when you go to take the test, remain confident and remember how well you did on the practice tests. If you can score high enough on a practice test, then you can do the same on the real thing.

General Strategies

The most important thing you can do is to ignore your fears and jump into the test immediately- do not be overwhelmed by any strange-sounding terms. You have to jump into the test like jumping into a pool- all at once is the easiest way.

Make Predictions

As you read and understand the question, try to guess what the answer will be. Remember that several of the answer choices are wrong, and once you begin reading them, your mind will immediately become cluttered with answer choices designed to throw you off. Your mind is typically the most focused immediately after you have read the question and digested its contents. If you can, try to predict what the correct answer will be. You may be surprised at what you can predict.

Quickly scan the choices and see if your prediction is in the listed answer choices. If it is, then you can be quite confident that you have the right answer. It still won't hurt to check the other answer choices, but most of the time, you've got it!

Answer the Question

It may seem obvious to only pick answer choices that answer the question, but the test writers can create some excellent answer choices that are wrong. Don't pick an answer just because it sounds right, or you believe it to be true. It MUST answer the question. Once you've made your selection, always go back and check it against the question and make sure that you didn't misread the question, and the answer choice does answer the question posed.

Benchmark

After you read the first answer choice, decide if you think it sounds correct or not. If it doesn't, move on to the next answer choice. If it does, mentally mark that answer choice. This doesn't mean that you've definitely selected it as your answer choice, it just means that it's the best you've seen thus far. Go ahead and read the next choice. If the next choice is worse than the one you've already selected, keep going to the next answer choice. If the next choice is better than the choice you've already selected, mentally mark the new answer choice as your best guess.

The first answer choice that you select becomes your standard. Every other answer choice must be benchmarked against that standard. That choice is correct until proven otherwise by another answer choice beating it out. Once you've decided that no other answer choice seems as good, do one final check to ensure that your answer choice answers the question posed.

Valid Information

Don't discount any of the information provided in the question. Every piece of information may be necessary to determine the correct answer. None of the information in the question is there to throw you off (while the answer choices will certainly have information to throw you off). If two seemingly unrelated topics are discussed, don't ignore either. You can be confident there is a relationship, or it wouldn't be included in the question, and you are probably going to have to determine what is that relationship to find the answer.

Avoid "Fact Traps"

Don't get distracted by a choice that is factually true. Your search is for the answer that answers the question. Stay focused and don't fall for an answer that is true but incorrect. Always go back to the question and make sure you're choosing an answer that actually answers the question and is not just a true statement. An answer can be factually correct, but it MUST answer the question asked. Additionally, two answers can both be seemingly correct, so be sure to read all of the answer choices, and make sure that you get the one that BEST answers the question.

Milk the Question

Some of the questions may throw you completely off. They might deal with a subject you have not been exposed to, or one that you haven't reviewed in years. While your lack of knowledge about the subject will be a hindrance, the question itself can give you many clues that will help you find the correct answer. Read the question carefully and look for clues. Watch particularly for adjectives and nouns describing difficult terms or words that you don't recognize. Regardless of if you completely understand a word or not, replacing it with a synonym either provided or one you more familiar with may help you to understand what the questions are asking. Rather than wracking your mind about specific detailed information concerning a difficult term or word, try to use mental substitutes that are easier to understand.

The Trap of Familiarity

Don't just choose a word because you recognize it. On difficult questions, you may not recognize a number of words in the answer choices. The test writers don't put "make-believe" words on the test; so don't think that just because you only recognize all the words in one answer choice means that answer choice must be correct. If you only recognize words in one answer choice, then focus on that one. Is it correct? Try your best to determine if it is correct. If it is, that is great, but if it doesn't, eliminate it. Each word and answer choice you eliminate increases your chances of getting the question correct, even if you then have to guess among the unfamiliar choices.

Eliminate Answers

Eliminate choices as soon as you realize they are wrong. But be careful! Make sure you consider all of the possible answer choices. Just because one appears right, doesn't mean that the next one won't be even better! The test writers will usually put more than one good answer choice for every question, so read all of them. Don't worry if you are stuck between two that seem right. By getting down to just two remaining possible choices, your odds are now 50/50. Rather than wasting too much time, play the odds. You are guessing, but guessing wisely, because you've been able to knock out some of the answer choices that you know are wrong. If you are eliminating choices and realize that the last answer choice you are left with is also obviously wrong, don't panic. Start over and consider each choice again. There may easily be something that you missed the first time and will realize on the second pass.

Tough Questions

If you are stumped on a problem or it appears too hard or too difficult, don't waste time. Move on! Remember though, if you can quickly check for obviously incorrect answer choices, your chances of guessing correctly are greatly improved. Before you completely give up, at least try to knock out a couple of possible answers. Eliminate what you can and then guess at the remaining answer choices before moving on.

Brainstorm

If you get stuck on a difficult question, spend a few seconds quickly brainstorming. Run through the complete list of possible answer choices. Look at each choice and ask yourself, "Could this answer the question satisfactorily?" Go through each answer choice and consider it independently of the other. By systematically going through all possibilities, you may find something that you would otherwise overlook. Remember that when you get stuck, it's important to try to keep moving.

Read Carefully

Understand the problem. Read the question and answer choices carefully. Don't miss the question because you misread the terms. You have plenty of time to read each question thoroughly and make sure you understand what is being asked. Yet a happy medium must be attained, so don't waste too much time. You must read carefully, but efficiently.

Face Value

When in doubt, use common sense. Always accept the situation in the problem at face value. Don't read too much into it. These problems will not require you to make huge leaps of logic. The test writers aren't trying to throw you off with a cheap trick. If you have to go beyond creativity and make a leap of logic in order to have an answer choice answer the question, then you should look at the other answer choices. Don't overcomplicate the problem by creating theoretical relationships or explanations that will warp time or space. These are normal problems rooted in reality. It's just that the applicable relationship or explanation may not be readily apparent and you have to figure things out. Use your common sense to interpret anything that isn't clear.

Prefixes

If you're having trouble with a word in the question or answer choices, try dissecting it. Take advantage of every clue that the word might include. Prefixes and suffixes can be a huge help. Usually they allow you to determine a basic meaning. Pre- means before, post- means after, pro - is positive, de- is negative. From these prefixes and suffixes, you can get an idea of the general meaning of the word and try to put it into context. Beware though of any traps. Just because con is the opposite of pro, doesn't necessarily mean congress is the opposite of progress!

Hedge Phrases

Watch out for critical "hedge" phrases, such as likely, may, can, will often, sometimes, often, almost, mostly, usually, generally, rarely, sometimes. Question writers insert these hedge phrases to cover every possibility. Often an answer choice will be wrong simply because it leaves no room for exception. Avoid answer choices that have definitive words like "exactly," and "always".

Switchback Words

Stay alert for "switchbacks". These are the words and phrases frequently used to alert you to shifts in thought. The most common switchback word is "but". Others include although, however, nevertheless, on the other hand, even though, while, in spite of, despite, regardless of.

New Information

Correct answer choices will rarely have completely new information included. Answer choices typically are straightforward reflections of the material asked about and will directly relate to the question. If a new piece of information is included in an answer choice that doesn't even seem to relate to the topic being asked about, then that answer choice is likely incorrect. All of the information needed to answer the question is usually provided for you, and so you should not have to make guesses that are unsupported or choose answer choices that require unknown information that cannot be reasoned on its own.

Time Management

On technical questions, don't get lost on the technical terms. Don't spend too much time on any one question. If you don't know what a term means, then since you don't have a dictionary, odds are you aren't going to get much further. You should immediately recognize terms as whether or not you know them. If you don't, work with the other clues that you have, the other answer choices and terms provided, but don't waste too much time trying to figure out a difficult term.

Contextual Clues

Look for contextual clues. An answer can be right but not correct. The contextual clues will help you find the answer that is most right and is correct. Understand the context in which a phrase or statement is made. This will help you make important distinctions.

Don't Panic

Panicking will not answer any questions for you. Therefore, it isn't helpful. When you first see the question, if your mind goes blank, take a deep breath. Force yourself to mechanically go through the steps of solving the problem and using the strategies you've learned.

Pace Yourself

Don't get clock fever. It's easy to be overwhelmed when you're looking at a page full of questions, your mind is full of random thoughts and feeling confused, and the clock is ticking down faster than you would like. Calm down and maintain the pace that you have set for yourself. As long as you are on track by monitoring your pace, you are guaranteed to have enough time for yourself. When you get to the last few minutes of the test, it may seem like you won't have enough time left, but if you only have as many questions as you should have left at that point, then you're right on track!

Answer Selection

The best way to pick an answer choice is to eliminate all of those that are wrong, until only one is left and confirm that is the correct answer. Sometimes though, an answer choice may immediately look right. Be careful! Take a second to make sure that the other choices are not equally obvious. Don't make a hasty mistake. There are only two times that you should stop before checking other answers. First is when you are positive that the answer choice you have selected is correct. Second is when time is almost out and you have to make a quick guess!

Check Your Work

Since you will probably not know every term listed and the answer to every question, it is important that you get credit for the ones that you do know. Don't miss any questions through careless mistakes. If at all possible, try to take a second to look back over your answer selection and make sure you've selected the correct answer choice and haven't made a costly careless mistake (such as marking an answer choice that you didn't mean to mark). This quick double check should more than pay for itself in caught mistakes for the time it costs.

Beware of Directly Quoted Answers

Sometimes an answer choice will repeat word for word a portion of the question or reference section. However, beware of such exact duplication – it may be a trap!

More than likely, the correct choice will paraphrase or summarize a point, rather than being exactly the same wording.

Slang

Scientific sounding answers are better than slang ones. An answer choice that begins "To compare the outcomes…" is much more likely to be correct than one that begins "Because some people insisted…"

Extreme Statements

Avoid wild answers that throw out highly controversial ideas that are proclaimed as established fact. An answer choice that states the "process should be used in certain situations, if…" is much more likely to be correct than one that states the "process should be discontinued completely." The first is a calm rational statement and doesn't even make a definitive, uncompromising stance, using a hedge word "if" to provide wiggle room, whereas the second choice is a radical idea and far more extreme.

Answer Choice Families

When you have two or more answer choices that are direct opposites or parallels, one of them is usually the correct answer. For instance, if one answer choice states "x increases" and another answer choice states "x decreases" or "y increases," then those two or three answer choices are very similar in construction and fall into the same family of answer choices. A family of answer choices is when two or three answer choices are very similar in construction, and yet often have a directly opposite meaning. Usually the correct answer choice will be in that family of answer choices. The "odd man out" or answer choice that doesn't seem to fit the parallel construction of the other answer choices is more likely to be incorrect.

Special Report: How to Overcome Test Anxiety

The very nature of tests caters to some level of anxiety, nervousness or tension, just as we feel for any important event that occurs in our lives. A little bit of anxiety or nervousness can be a good thing. It helps us with motivation, and makes achievement just that much sweeter. However, too much anxiety can be a problem; especially if it hinders our ability to function and perform.

"Test anxiety," is the term that refers to the emotional reactions that some test-takers experience when faced with a test or exam. Having a fear of testing and exams is based upon a rational fear, since the test-taker's performance can shape the course of an academic career. Nevertheless, experiencing excessive fear of examinations will only interfere with the test-takers ability to perform, and his/her chances to be successful.

There are a large variety of causes that can contribute to the development and sensation of test anxiety. These include, but are not limited to lack of performance and worrying about issues surrounding the test.

Lack of Preparation

Lack of preparation can be identified by the following behaviors or situations:

Not scheduling enough time to study, and therefore cramming the night before the test or exam

Managing time poorly, to create the sensation that there is not enough time to do everything

Failing to organize the text information in advance, so that the study material consists of the entire text and not simply the pertinent information

Poor overall studying habits

Worrying, on the other hand, can be related to both the test taker, or many other factors around him/her that will be affected by the results of the test. These include worrying about:

Previous performances on similar exams, or exams in general

How friends and other students are achieving

The negative consequences that will result from a poor grade or failure

There are three primary elements to test anxiety. Physical components, which involve the same typical bodily reactions as those to acute anxiety (to be discussed below). Emotional factors have to do with fear or panic. Mental or cognitive issues concerning attention spans and memory abilities.

Physical Signals

There are many different symptoms of test anxiety, and these are not limited to mental and emotional strain. Frequently there are a range of physical signals that will let a test taker know that he/she is suffering from test anxiety. These bodily changes can include the following:

Perspiring
Sweaty palms
Wet, trembling hands
Nausea
Dry mouth
A knot in the stomach
Headache
Faintness
Muscle tension
Aching shoulders, back and neck
Rapid heart beat
Feeling too hot/cold

To recognize the sensation of test anxiety, a test-taker should monitor him/herself for the following sensations:

The physical distress symptoms as listed above
Emotional sensitivity, expressing emotional feelings such as the need to cry or laugh too much, or a sensation of anger or helplessness
A decreased ability to think, causing the test-taker to blank out or have racing thoughts that are hard to organize or control.

Though most students will feel some level of anxiety when faced with a test or exam, the majority can cope with that anxiety and maintain it at a manageable level. However, those who cannot are faced with a very real and very serious condition, which can and should be controlled for the immeasurable benefit of this sufferer.

Naturally, these sensations lead to negative results for the testing experience. The most common effects of test anxiety have to do with nervousness and mental blocking.

Nervousness

Nervousness can appear in several different levels:

The test-taker's difficulty, or even inability to read and understand the questions on the test
The difficulty or inability to organize thoughts to a coherent form
The difficulty or inability to recall key words and concepts relating to the testing questions (especially essays)
The receipt of poor grades on a test, though the test material was well known by the test taker
Conversely, a person may also experience mental blocking, which involves:

Blanking out on test questions
Only remembering the correct answers to the questions when the test has already finished.

Fortunately for test anxiety sufferers, beating these feelings, to a large degree, has to do with proper preparation. When a test taker has a feeling of preparedness, then anxiety will be dramatically lessened.

The first step to resolving anxiety issues is to distinguish which of the two types of anxiety are being suffered. If the anxiety is a direct result of a lack of preparation, this should be considered a normal reaction, and the anxiety level (as opposed to the test results) shouldn't be anything to worry about. However, if, when adequately prepared, the test-taker still panics, blanks out, or seems to overreact, this is not a fully rational reaction. While this can be considered normal too, there are many ways to combat and overcome these effects.

Remember that anxiety cannot be entirely eliminated, however, there are ways to minimize it, to make the anxiety easier to manage. Preparation is one of the best ways to minimize test anxiety. Therefore the following techniques are wise in order to best fight off any anxiety that may want to build.

To begin with, try to avoid cramming before a test, whenever it is possible. By trying to memorize an entire term's worth of information in one day, you'll be shocking your system, and not giving yourself a very good chance to absorb the information. This is an easy path to anxiety, so for those who suffer from test anxiety, cramming should not even be considered an option.

Instead of cramming, work throughout the semester to combine all of the material which is presented throughout the semester, and work on it gradually as the course goes by, making sure to master the main concepts first, leaving minor details for a week or so before the test.

To study for the upcoming exam, be sure to pose questions that may be on the examination, to gauge the ability to answer them by integrating the ideas from your texts, notes and lectures, as well as any supplementary readings.

If it is truly impossible to cover all of the information that was covered in that particular term, concentrate on the most important portions, that can be covered very well. Learn these concepts as best as possible, so that when the test comes, a goal can be made to use these concepts as presentations of your knowledge.

In addition to study habits, changes in attitude are critical to beating a struggle with test anxiety. In fact, an improvement of the perspective over the entire test-taking experience can actually help a test taker to enjoy studying and therefore improve the overall experience. Be certain not to overemphasize the significance of the grade - know that the result of the test is neither a reflection of self worth, nor is it a measure of intelligence; one grade will not predict a person's future success.

To improve an overall testing outlook, the following steps should be tried:

Keeping in mind that the most reasonable expectation for taking a test is to expect to try to demonstrate as much of what you know as you possibly can.

Reminding ourselves that a test is only one test; this is not the only one, and there will be others.

The thought of thinking of oneself in an irrational, all-or-nothing term should be avoided at all costs.

A reward should be designated for after the test, so there's something to look forward to. Whether it be going to a movie, going out to eat, or simply visiting friends, schedule it in advance, and do it no matter what result is expected on the exam.

Test-takers should also keep in mind that the basics are some of the most important things, even beyond anti-anxiety techniques and studying. Never neglect the basic social, emotional and biological needs, in order to try to absorb information. In order to best achieve, these three factors must be held as just as important as the studying itself.

Study Steps

Remember the following important steps for studying:

Maintain healthy nutrition and exercise habits. Continue both your recreational activities and social pass times. These both contribute to your physical and emotional well being.

Be certain to get a good amount of sleep, especially the night before the test, because when you're overtired you are not able to perform to the best of your best ability.

Keep the studying pace to a moderate level by taking breaks when they are needed, and varying the work whenever possible, to keep the mind fresh instead of getting bored.

When enough studying has been done that all the material that can be learned has been learned, and the test taker is prepared for the test, stop studying and do something relaxing such as listening to music, watching a movie, or taking a warm bubble bath.

There are also many other techniques to minimize the uneasiness or apprehension that is experienced along with test anxiety before, during, or even after the examination. In fact, there are a great deal of things that can be done to stop anxiety from interfering with lifestyle and performance. Again, remember that anxiety will not be eliminated entirely, and it shouldn't be. Otherwise that "up" feeling for exams would not exist, and most of us depend on that sensation to perform better than usual. However, this anxiety has to be at a level that is manageable.

Of course, as we have just discussed, being prepared for the exam is half the battle right away. Attending all classes, finding out what knowledge will be expected on the exam, and knowing the exam schedules are easy steps to lowering anxiety. Keeping up with work will remove the need to cram, and efficient study habits will eliminate wasted time. Studying should be done in an ideal location for concentration, so that it is simple to become interested in the material and give it complete attention. A method such as SQ3R (Survey, Question, Read, Recite, Review) is a wonderful key to follow to make sure that the study habits are as effective as possible, especially in the case of learning from a textbook. Flashcards are great techniques for memorization. Learning to take good notes will mean that notes will be full of useful information, so that less sifting will need to be done to seek out what is pertinent for studying. Reviewing notes after class and then again on occasion will keep the information fresh in the mind. From notes that have been taken summary sheets and outlines can be made for simpler reviewing.

A study group can also be a very motivational and helpful place to study, as there will be a sharing of ideas, all of the minds can work together, to make sure that everyone understands, and the studying will be made more interesting because it will be a social occasion.

Basically, though, as long as the test-taker remains organized and self confident, with efficient study habits, less time will need to be spent studying, and higher grades will be achieved.

To become self confident, there are many useful steps. The first of these is "self talk." It has been shown through extensive research, that self-talk for students who suffer from test anxiety, should be well monitored, in order to make sure that it contributes to self confidence as opposed to sinking the student. Frequently the self talk of test-anxious students is negative or self-defeating, thinking that everyone else is smarter and faster, that they always mess up, and that if they don't do well, they'll fail the entire course. It is important to decreasing anxiety that awareness is made of self talk. Try writing any negative self thoughts and then disputing them with a positive statement instead. Begin self-encouragement as though it was a friend speaking. Repeat positive statements to help reprogram the mind to believing in successes instead of failures.

Helpful Techniques

Other extremely helpful techniques include:

Self-visualization of doing well and reaching goals

While aiming for an "A" level of understanding, don't try to "overprotect" by setting your expectations lower. This will only convince the mind to stop studying in order to meet the lower expectations.

Don't make comparisons with the results or habits of other students. These are individual factors, and different things work for different people, causing different results.

Strive to become an expert in learning what works well, and what can be done in order to improve. Consider collecting this data in a journal.
Create rewards for after studying instead of doing things before studying that will only turn into avoidance behaviors.

Make a practice of relaxing - by using methods such as progressive relaxation, self-hypnosis, guided imagery, etc - in order to make relaxation an automatic sensation.

Work on creating a state of relaxed concentration so that concentrating will take on the focus of the mind, so that none will be wasted on worrying.

Take good care of the physical self by eating well and getting enough sleep.

Plan in time for exercise and stick to this plan.

Beyond these techniques, there are other methods to be used before, during and after the test that will help the test-taker perform well in addition to overcoming anxiety.

Before the exam comes the academic preparation. This involves establishing a study schedule and beginning at least one week before the actual date of the test. By doing this, the anxiety of not having enough time to study for the test will be automatically eliminated. Moreover, this will make the studying a much more effective experience, ensuring that the learning will be an easier process. This relieves much undue pressure on the test-taker.

Summary sheets, note cards, and flash cards with the main concepts and examples of these main concepts should be prepared in advance of the actual studying time. A topic should never be eliminated from this process. By omitting a topic because it isn't expected to be on the test is only setting up the test-taker for anxiety should it actually appear on the exam. Utilize the course syllabus for laying out the topics that should be studied. Carefully go over the notes that were made in class, paying special attention to any of the issues that the professor took special care to emphasize while lecturing in class. In the textbooks, use the chapter review, or if possible, the chapter tests, to begin your review.

It may even be possible to ask the instructor what information will be covered on the exam, or what the format of the exam will be (for example, multiple choice, essay, free form, true-false). Additionally, see if it is possible to find out how many questions will be on the test. If a review sheet or sample test has been offered by the professor, make good use of it, above anything else, for the preparation for the test. Another great resource for getting to know the examination is reviewing tests from previous semesters. Use these tests to review, and aim to achieve a 100% score on each of the possible topics. With a few exceptions, the goal that you set for yourself is the highest one that you will reach.

Take all of the questions that were assigned as homework, and rework them to any other possible course material. The more problems reworked, the more skill and confidence will form as a result. When forming the solution to a problem, write out each of the steps. Don't simply do head work. By doing as many steps on paper as possible, much clarification and therefore confidence will be formed. Do this with as many homework problems as possible, before checking the answers. By checking the answer after each problem, a reinforcement will exist, that will not be on the exam. Study situations should be as exam-like as possible, to prime the test-taker's system for the experience. By waiting to check the answers at the end, a psychological advantage will be formed, to decrease the stress factor.

Another fantastic reason for not cramming is the avoidance of confusion in concepts, especially when it comes to mathematics. 8-10 hours of study will become one hundred percent more effective if it is spread out over a week or at least several days, instead of doing it all in one sitting. Recognize that the human brain requires time in order to assimilate new material, so frequent breaks and a span of study time over several days will be much more beneficial.

Additionally, don't study right up until the point of the exam. Studying should stop a minimum of one hour before the exam begins. This allows the brain to rest and put things in their proper order. This will also provide the time to become as relaxed as possible when going into the examination room. The test-taker will also have time to eat well and eat sensibly. Know that the brain needs food as much as the rest of the body. With enough food and enough sleep, as well as a relaxed attitude, the body and the mind are primed for success.

Avoid any anxious classmates who are talking about the exam. These students only spread anxiety, and are not worth sharing the anxious sentimentalities.

Before the test also involves creating a positive attitude, so mental preparation should also be a point of concentration. There are many keys to creating a positive attitude. Should fears become rushing in, make a visualization of taking the exam, doing well, and seeing an A written on the paper. Write out a list of affirmations that will bring a feeling of confidence, such as "I am doing well in my English class," "I studied well and know my material," "I enjoy this class." Even if the affirmations aren't believed at first, it sends a positive message to the subconscious which will result in an alteration of the overall belief system, which is the system that creates reality.

If a sensation of panic begins, work with the fear and imagine the very worst! Work through the entire scenario of not passing the test, failing the entire course, and dropping out of school, followed by not getting a job, and pushing a shopping cart through the dark alley where you'll live. This will place things into perspective! Then, practice deep breathing and create a visualization of the opposite situation - achieving an "A" on the exam, passing the entire course, receiving the degree at a graduation ceremony.

On the day of the test, there are many things to be done to ensure the best results, as well as the most calm outlook. The following stages are suggested in order to maximize test-taking potential:

Begin the examination day with a moderate breakfast, and avoid any coffee or beverages with caffeine if the test taker is prone to jitters. Even people who are used to managing caffeine can feel jittery or light-headed when it is taken on a test day.

Attempt to do something that is relaxing before the examination begins. As last minute cramming clouds the mastering of overall concepts, it is better to use this time to create a calming outlook.

Be certain to arrive at the test location well in advance, in order to provide time to select a location that is away from doors, windows and other distractions, as well as giving enough time to relax before the test begins.

Keep away from anxiety generating classmates who will upset the sensation of stability and relaxation that is being attempted before the exam.

Should the waiting period before the exam begins cause anxiety, create a self-distraction by reading a light magazine or something else that is relaxing and simple.

During the exam itself, read the entire exam from beginning to end, and find out how much time should be allotted to each individual problem. Once writing the exam, should more time be taken for a problem, it should be abandoned, in order to begin another problem. If there is time at the end, the unfinished problem can always be returned to and completed.

Read the instructions very carefully - twice - so that unpleasant surprises won't follow during or after the exam has ended.

When writing the exam, pretend that the situation is actually simply the completion of homework within a library, or at home. This will assist in forming a relaxed atmosphere, and will allow the brain extra focus for the complex thinking function.

Begin the exam with all of the questions with which the most confidence is felt. This will build the confidence level regarding the entire exam and will begin a quality momentum. This will also create encouragement for trying the problems where uncertainty resides.

Going with the "gut instinct" is always the way to go when solving a problem. Second guessing should be avoided at all costs. Have confidence in the ability to do well.

For essay questions, create an outline in advance that will keep the mind organized and make certain that all of the points are remembered. For multiple choice, read every answer, even if the correct one has been spotted - a better one may exist.

Continue at a pace that is reasonable and not rushed, in order to be able to work carefully. Provide enough time to go over the answers at the end, to check for small errors that can be corrected.

Should a feeling of panic begin, breathe deeply, and think of the feeling of the body releasing sand through its pores. Visualize a calm, peaceful place, and include all of the sights, sounds and sensations of this image. Continue the deep breathing, and take a few minutes to continue this with closed eyes. When all is well again, return to the test.

If a "blanking" occurs for a certain question, skip it and move on to the next question. There will be time to return to the other question later. Get everything done that can be done, first, to guarantee all the grades that can be compiled, and to build all of the confidence possible. Then return to the weaker questions to build the marks from there.

Remember, one's own reality can be created, so as long as the belief is there, success will follow. And remember: anxiety can happen later, right now, there's an exam to be written!

After the examination is complete, whether there is a feeling for a good grade or a bad grade, don't dwell on the exam, and be certain to follow through on the reward that was promised...and enjoy it! Don't dwell on any mistakes that have been made, as there is nothing that can be done at this point anyway.

Additionally, don't begin to study for the next test right away. Do something relaxing for a while, and let the mind relax and prepare itself to begin absorbing information again.

From the results of the exam - both the grade and the entire experience, be certain to learn from what has gone on. Perfect studying habits and work some more on confidence in order to make the next examination experience even better than the last one.

Learn to avoid places where openings occurred for laziness, procrastination and day dreaming.

Use the time between this exam and the next one to better learn to relax, even learning to relax on cue, so that any anxiety can be controlled during the next exam. Learn how to relax the body. Slouch in your chair if that helps. Tighten and then relax all of the different muscle groups, one group at a time, beginning with the feet and then working all the way up to the neck and face. This will ultimately relax the muscles more than they were to begin with. Learn how to breathe deeply and comfortably, and focus on this breathing going in and out as a relaxing thought. With every exhale, repeat the word "relax."

As common as test anxiety is, it is very possible to overcome it. Make yourself one of the test-takers who overcome this frustrating hindrance.

Special Report: Additional Bonus Material

Due to our efforts to try to keep this book to a manageable length, we've created a link that will give you access to all of your additional bonus material.

Please visit http://www.mometrix.com/bonus948/ace to access the information.